# HOW TO
# FRANCHISE YOUR
# BUSINESS

The
Canadian Franchise Association's
Official "How-To" Guide
On Franchising Your Business

# HOW TO FRANCHISE YOUR BUSINESS

## The Canadian Franchise Association's Official "How-To" Guide On Franchising Your Business

Canadian Franchise Association

2585 Skymark Avenue, Suite # 300
Mississauga Ontario
L4W 4L5

Phone: 905-625-2896 or 800-665-4232
Website: www.cfa.ca

**HOW TO FRANCHISE YOUR BUSINESS**
The Canadian Franchise Association's Official
"How To" Guide On Franchising Your Business

**Copyright © 2002, Canadian Franchise Association**

**Published in 2002 by**

Canadian Franchise Association
2585 Skymark Avenue, Suite # 300
Mississauga Ontario L4W 4L5

ISBN 0-9730605-0-6

**Important Disclaimer**: This publication is sold with the understanding that (1) the Canadian Franchise Association (the "publisher"), authors and editors are not responsible for the results of any actions taken on the basis of information in this work, nor for any errors or omissions; and (2) the publisher, authors and editors are not, in this publication, engaged in rendering legal, accounting or other professional services. The publisher, authors and editors, expressly disclaim all and any liability to any person, whether a purchaser of this publication or not, in respect of anything and of the consequences of anything done or omitted to be done by any such person in reliance, whether whole or partial, upon the whole or any part of the contents of this publication. The views of the authors are not neccessarily those of the publishers and/or the editors. If legal advice or other expert assistance is required, the services of a competent professional person should be sought.

*Cover design & layout by Cary Eveline*

*Printed and bound in Canada*

# TABLE OF CONTENTS

## PREFACE

## CHAPTER 1

### Starting A Franchise Family

## CHAPTER 2

### The Financial Aspects Of Becoming A Franchisor

# Chapter 3

## The Legal Aspects Of Becoming A Franchisor

## CHAPTER 4

### An Overview Of Canadian Franchise Laws

## CHAPTER 5

### Intellectual Property In Franchising

# CHAPTER 6

# Marketing your Franchises - A Primer

## CHAPTER 7

### One Franchisor's Journey

## ABOUT THE AUTHORS

# PREFACE

# MESSAGE FROM THE CANADIAN FRANCHISE ASSOCIATION

*By:Richard Cunningham*
*President & CEO,*
*Canadian Franchise Association*

One of the most frequently asked questions heard at the Canadian Franchise Association is "how do I franchise my business?" This book was brought about through the efforts of a dedicated group of volunteers, Canadian Franchise Association members, and employees, to respond to that question. We want entrepreneurs to know the right steps to build a successful and profitable franchise network from the bricks and mortar of their own small business—specifically, a franchise that will enhance and protect the investments of all parties, both franchisors and franchisees.

I have an intimate understanding of what it means to start and grow your own business. Before becoming the president of the CFA, I owned several small businesses. Running my own business taught me the value of hard work and personal commitment. I have an appreciation for other business people who have invested their money, time and sweat into a profitable business venture because I lived through the risks and sacrifices it took to make an independent business succeed.

In my role as the President & CEO of the CFA I have seen first hand how demanding the transition from small independent business owner to franchisor can be. The history of franchising in Canada is full of well-known success stories. Most Canadians are familiar with the franchise businesses that are represented on the main streets and in the malls in every city and town across the country. And all of the Canadian chains that operate hundreds, and sometimes thousands, of locations not just in Canada but around the world all began with one store, one concept and an entrepreneur that made it happen. Tim Hortons, Harvey's, Swiss Chalet, Boston Pizza, M&M Meat Shops, The Keg, and Shoppers Drug Mart, the list of born and bred Canadian businesses that have used the franchise format to achieve astounding success reads like a role call for the Canadian small-business Hall of Fame.

That being said, franchising also presents unique challenges to entrepreneurs interested in expanding their business. Certainly, franchising allows a business to grow at a rate that is very rarely achieved through a completely corporate or private operational format. However, it also changes the very nature of the business. At some point in the process, every franchisor who is serious about making an impact in the industry must come to terms with the fact that their primary concern is no longer manning the front lines of the business that they loved and nurtured—be it retailer or restauranteur—but rather the management and expansion of the franchise network. Finding qualified franchisees, keeping existing franchisees happy, running an effective head office, keeping the brand fresh, scouting new markets, these are the issues that franchisors are dealing with on a daily basis. And, while in many instances these business people have risen to the challenge and prospered, many franchisors have realized that the skill sets needed to get through the transition are foreign to them.

In many cases, not having a solid plan for growth and sticking to it has been at the root of franchises that flounder. The lure of people waving cheques and wanting copies of your marketing materials can be a temptation for young franchise systems that is difficult to resist. Unfortunately, some of the worst abuses have belonged to businesses that develop a concept only so that it can be mass marketed through franchising. The use of franchising to expand a business must be done based on a successful model.

The CFA believes that building mutually beneficial and rewarding relationships with qualified and talented franchisees is at the heart of success in this industry. Finding those people who are a perfect match for your system takes time but pays off. You will need to replicate your own passion for your business and desire to succeed in each franchisee that invests in your concept. I also think one of the most difficult problems franchisors have, is to manage the expectations of potential franchisees. Just as new franchisors need to understand that success comes with hard work, your franchisees need to put all of their energy into making their own stores work—they need to know that their rewards are not automatic. The easy part is teaching them how to make a doughnut, rent a car or paint houses but the tougher part is convincing them to like it.

This book draws from the experience of franchise professionals who are among the best of the franchise industry in their respective fields. The two franchisors who contributed chapters to this book, Kent Harding founder of Kwik Kopy Printing Canada and Mac Voisin of M&M Meat Shops, established their businesses and built their brands without the support and resources that exist for up-and-coming businesses in the franchise community today. As pioneers in the field, the advice they offer is based on decades of trial and error, turning their enterprises into two of the best known and trusted businesses in Canada. We also drew upon the expertise of top franchise lawyers, accountants and brokers from some of Canada's most established firms for their insight into the pressing issues fledgling franchisors need to know about to manage franchise expansion. This valuable information will help business people from any background take the first steps toward a well-planned franchise future.

The Canadian Franchise Association is the nation's only trade association representing the shared interests of all stakeholders working in the franchise industry. Our members include established businesses that are synonymous with franchising to the Canadian public, as well as businesses who are just learning the ropes—including a few that have yet to sell their first franchise. Involvement in the CFA and networking with your peers is a great way to learn what sets a prospering franchise network apart.

By joining the CFA, new members rub elbows with veteran franchise professionals who have seen it all in the industry. Plus, the association includes the top affiliated professionals - the bankers, lawyers, accountants and brokers who all franchisors need to know to get the best advice if they are going to get ahead. And forging business connections with the dominant players in the industry help members build their own reputation within the franchise community. Membership in the CFA shows your franchisees that you are serious about establishing yourself among franchising's business leaders.

I once had a successful franchisor tell me that the greatest achievement for him was to realize his own dreams by helping his franchisees achieve theirs. Good luck in all your business ventures and the realization of all your dreams.

# CHAIRMAN'S MESSAGE

*By: Sam Hamam,*
*President & CEO*
*Motophoto Canada*

If you are reading this message, then it is likely that you are considering whether to adopt franchising as a method of distributing your products or services. This book will assist you in making the determination as to whether franchising is right for you, and your business. So, the purpose of my message is not to repeat the material that you will find in this work, but to simply relay how franchising enabled me, and my own family, to succeed and prosper.

As the last 30 plus years have shown, franchising is an important engine in today's retail and service economies. The spread of many, if not most, brand name chains has depended on the ability to replicate the concept across vast geographic areas in a relatively short period of time. This has been achieved through tapping into the great market of entrepreneurs across North America. For the most part these are people who simply want to be in business for themselves, but chose to purchase a franchise, so that they would not be in business by themselves. With their access to franchisees' capital many of the biggest brand name chains took off, and now dot the landscape. They succeed by being able to offer an ever increasing and mobile population a familiar product, taste or service.

After working for twenty years in the field of engineering, both overseas and in Canada, I felt it was time to take charge of my own destiny. To do so I decided it was time to own my own business. Despite my entrepreneurial drive, I quickly realized that starting a business from scratch is a risky venture that I was not prepared to take at that stage in my life. Franchising seemed to be the perfect middle of the road approach for me to pursue, since it gave me the independence I needed, and simultaneously satisfied my entrepreneurial drive, all without exposing me to undue risk that would keep me awake all night.

In 1987, my brothers and I decided to acquire the master franchise rights for Ontario, and subsequently Canada, from the American based MotoPhoto chain. We started as franchisees, by opening our first store, then set about to start franchising our chain. Being both franchisee and franchisor, I believe, has given me and my franchise system a unique perspective on the nature of the relationships that are so important for a franchised business to succeed. Today we oversee a system of approximately 35 franchised and corporate Motophoto stores in this country. In addition there are another 350 plus outlets in the United States.

When we began our journey, there was little in the way of written material to assist. We quickly decided that membership in the Canadian Franchise Association, and our network of contacts and professionals, could serve as valuable resources. Nevertheless, we never had the benefit of a book such as this one, that provides valuable insight and information to assist

Canadian business people understand the rewards and challenges that face them when they begin a franchise expansion program.

I am extremely proud that this work could be made available at this time. It is especially timely for another reason, as it coincides with the beginning of my tenure as Chairman of the Canadian Franchise Association. It will make my job as Chairman that much easier, as the CFA continues with its mandate of promoting quality, and ethical franchising. I commend the authors, editors, and CFA staff, for being able to bring this important educational project to fruition.

Good luck to you, and I trust you will find this book both informative and helpful.

# EDITORS' ACKNOWLEDGEMENTS

Three years ago, the CFA asked its Communications Committee, chaired by Sherry MacLauchlan of McDonald's Restaurants of Canada Limited, to investigate the possibility of creating a book to educate individuals and companies on franchising as a method of doing business.

Upon taking on this mandate, the Communications Committee agreed that many of its members would contribute their experiences towards this book. The editors, and the professionals who are contributors to this work, were all members of that Committee.

The next step was to identify several successful Canadian franchisors to talk about their own growth strategies, and who could thus serve as role models for any business. Fortunately we were able to persuade both Kent Harding, founder of Kwik Kopy Printing in Canada, and Mac Voisin, founder of M&M Meat Shops, to contribute their words and thoughts.

The task of coordinating the efforts of so many contributors is no easy task. However, the job has now been completed. We have been fortunate to have the contribution, support and assistance of many talented individuals, including most notably Kim Divell, Chris McLean and Cary Eveline, all staff members of the Canadian Franchise Association. Of course, this work would not have been possible without the ongoing support of the CFA's President, Mr. Richard Cunningham, and the various members of the CFA's Executive.

To all those who contributed and assisted in bringing about this work, thank you.

We hope you will enjoy this overview of the road to becoming a franchisor.

Larry Weinberg and John Woodburn
March 2002

# CHAPTER 1

*By: Mac Voisin,*
*Co-founder and President*
*M&M Meat Shops*

## STARTING A FRANCHISE FAMILY

### INTRODUCTION

The world of the successful franchisor is filled with excitement, satisfaction, financial rewards and everyday fun....while the world of the unsuccessful franchisor is a very unpleasant one. Typically, an individual starts a business, builds it into a financially sound business venture and is then faced with the big decision – "Should I expand the business using a franchise business format, or should I simply own and operate a number of outlets? Should I expand my business through a combination of these two options?"

Unfortunately, there is no easy answer. Before making any decision, entrepreneurs must have a crystal clear understanding of their own strengths and weaknesses. Aspiring entrepreneurs will be influenced by the early successes of the business and believe that they can "conquer the world!"

Very often, these entrepreneurial skills are very different than the management skills necessary to successfully build a franchise business. This does not mean that the entrepreneur cannot play an active role in the franchise company. However, the person who built the business will have to evaluate what role he or she will play in the company.

It should also be clearly understood that the new franchisor will have to defer financial rewards during the early years, because any profits will have to be re-invested in the business. Once established, the financial payback to the franchisor can be significant.

Successful franchisors are always focused on the systematic, organized construction of their franchised business. Financial rewards are the by-product and final measurement gauge of the overall success of the franchised operation.

## FRANCHISING AND THE ECONOMY

Franchising has enjoyed tremendous growth over the past 25 to 30 years, and every year more and more consumer dollars are finding their way into franchised businesses. It is estimated that some $90 billion is spent in franchised outlets every year, so the impact on the Canadian economy is very substantial. Although most people think about fast food when they think about franchising, the reality is that franchising has permeated virtually every type of business imaginable, e.g.

- Accounting
- Advertising
- Auto products and services

- Building products and services
- Business services
- Car rentals
- Entertainment – movies –  video games
- Food
- Hotels, motels, campgrounds
- Lawn care
- Maid and janitorial services
- Personnel services
- Pet stores
- Printing; copying
- Security
- Telecommunications
- Travel
- etc., etc.

The Canadian Franchise Association estimates that there are currently over 1,200 franchised brands in Canada, conducting business in 44 different industries, operating over 75,000 outlets!

Each year many qualified candidates consider buying a franchise. For many, it's a way to escape the big boardrooms and find that perfect opportunity to be in a business for themselves but not by themselves. The security of operating under the franchise umbrella, plus the high probability for success in a franchise environment, are the key reasons for the growth of franchising.

## WHAT IS FRANCHISING?

Over the past several decades, franchising has emerged as the dominant small-business strategy for distributing products and services. For a wide variety of reasons, franchised companies know how to get and keep more customers than independent businesses. Franchisors do the research and they have the resources to rapidly expand the business. And because franchisees often invest large personal capital into the franchised business, they are much more committed to the ultimate success of the business than are most store managers.

A business is successful if it does two things very well – first, it must attract new customers to use its products and services and second, it must keep customers once they use the product or service.

Successful franchisors:

- design marketing programs that generate customers for the franchisee;

- offer a proven operating system that emphasizes superlative customer service;

- provides ongoing support to help franchisees retain customers

Simply put, franchising is a business strategy that is used to capture a dominant share of any market segment. Consumer loyalty is established when the franchisor develops proven operational guidelines and the franchisees in turn deliver their goods or services with consistency and quality. This results in a culture that promotes trust in brands. Consumers today have a strong love, even dependence, on brand loyalty.

*Consumer loyalty is established when the franchisor develops proven operational guidelines and the franchisees in turn deliver their goods or services with consistency and quality.*

For decades, franchising has enjoyed unprecedented growth and shows no signs of letting up. Franchisees are strong contributors to the communities in which they do business, and are among the most important sources for new business start-ups and job creation. Today, franchising is reportedly capturing 50 cents of every retail- and service-dollar spent by consumers.

More and more businesses are coming to realize that their profits can be enhanced and their costs reduced by using franchising instead of expensive company owned operations to capture market share. For several reasons, most franchised companies own one or many corporate stores. It's interesting to note that when units are converted to franchised outlets, sales increases are often very dramatic. At M&M Meat Shops, we have often built and owned stores until we find a suitable franchisee. In every case, the new franchisee has immediately enjoyed a 20 to 40% increase in sales. The franchisee is usually well known in the community and consumers are apt to be more supportive of the business that's locally owned and operated.

In franchising, the company ("franchisor") grants by contract to an individual or another company ("franchisee") the right to carry on a business in a prescribed way, in a particular location, for a specified period. The franchisee may be allowed to operate only one establishment or may be given an area in which a number of franchised outlets may be operated. For the services that it provides, the franchisor receives a fee or royalty – usually based on gross sales – or else a fixed fee.

In order to be successful, franchisors must be deeply committed to the success of their franchisees and the strengthening of their franchising programs. They must carefully select the right franchisees and then provide training, operational, marketing and support staff.

In the franchise development years – say the 1960s, '70s and '80s – many franchisors simply signed contracts with anyone who had the cash investment to take a franchise. They later discovered that many of these individuals simply didn't belong in a franchise environment. There was no attempt made to selectively ensure that only the right people were invited to join the franchise team. It is the "quality" and not the "quantity" of franchisees that will ultimately determine the success or failure of the franchise. Today, most franchisors understand the importance of establishing effective communications with their franchisees. Franchisors are soliciting the input of their franchisees in all areas of the business. They're setting up Advisory or Marketing Councils, Operations and Renovations Committees, etc., etc. More and more, franchisors and franchisees are coming to realize that they can build the business together in a non-confrontational atmosphere.

A successful franchising program is never based on luck, but rather an understanding of some of the components that build a solid foundation; i.e.

- franchisors have to continually reinvest in the business in order to reap long-term rewards. They need to have long-term vision by postponing short-term benefits;

- a proven prototype location (or chain of stores) that serve as the basis for the franchising program. The store (or stores) must have been tested, refined and operated successfully and be consistently profitable;

- a dedicated and committed ownership team that understands the industry plus the legal and business aspects of franchising as a method of doing business. As the business grows, the franchisor needs to build the team by hiring key personnel in all aspects of the operation – this includes marketing and operations people, financial and computer specialists, etc. Unfortunately, every business is different and so there is no blueprint of who to hire first;

- distinctive and registered trademarks, as well as consistent signage, slogans, uniforms and overall image. This is important in order to create corporate recognition of the brand;

- sufficient capitalization to launch and sustain the franchising program in order to provide initial and ongoing support to franchisees. The franchisor needs capital to pay for a comprehensive franchise agreement, franchise disclosure document, marketing brochures, etc.;

- proven methods of operation incorporated in operations manuals, initial and ongoing training programs. Ultimately, a complete set of management manuals must be prepared in order to assist franchisees in all areas of operation;

- field support staff who are skilled trainers and communicators and who can visit and assist franchisees and monitor quality control standards. The trainers need to have people and business skills, and a keen knowledge of what it takes to build the business. In some franchised companies, they are former franchisees, but this is not critical to the success of the field consulting;

- a well-drafted and forward thinking franchise agreement that balances the rights and obligations of franchisor and franchisee;

- a market demand for the products and services developed by the franchisor that will be distributed through the franchisees;

- site selection, demographic criteria and architectural standards;

- a genuine understanding of the competition;

- a franchisee profile and testing/screening system that places strong emphasis on licensing the right franchisees;

- an effective system of reporting and record keeping to maintain and monitor the performance of franchisees;

- a communication system that promotes ongoing meaningful dialogue with franchisees. Most franchisors set up an Advisory Council that has two essential purposes – first, it is a sounding board for proposed changes to the business by the franchisor and, second, to field ideas and criticisms from the franchisees;

- strong relationships with suppliers, lenders, and real estate developers. In the early years of the business, the franchisor needs to depend on external sources for advice and support, such as financial, marketing, real estate, etc. As the company grows, these experts can be put on the corporate payroll;

- research and development capabilities. In the early years of development, research and development is far from sophisticated. Much of it will come from one-on-one contact with customers. Listening to the wants and needs of customers will give direction to the franchisor for products and services

These are just some of the components required to build a firm foundation.

Most franchisors agree that most problems between the franchisor and franchisee are the result of a lack of shared understanding or shared meaning about the relationship. Consequently, the ability to develop a relationship based on solid communication is very important. Understanding the role and intent of each party in the relationship is key to building a successful relationship.

In a franchised business, the franchisor's business partner is the franchisee. The franchisor has to provide the tools necessary to the franchisee to properly serve/service the final purchaser of the product. Hence, the franchisor has a dual role in the relationship.

## TO FRANCHISE OR NOT TO FRANCHISE?

The decision 'to franchise or not to franchise' is usually made when the company is relatively new or small – perhaps one or several units only. This is not to say that larger companies with 50 to 100 corporately owned units don't decide to shift gears and enter the world of franchising. They do, but by and large, it's companies in their infancy that begin to consider the franchise alternative.

Before making the final commitment to franchise, the entrepreneur has to understand that the franchise business is totally different than the underlying business (such as hamburgers, transmission repairs, and lawn care). Hence, a franchisor is in two businesses, and successful franchisors are successful in both. Prospective franchisors must have a very clear, very accurate assessment of their own abilities and limitations. To be in the franchise business is to be in the 'people' business. In a sense, your customers are your franchisees and their customers are the people buying the product or service being offered by the core business. So managing people will be critical to the ultimate success of the franchised business.

In October 1980, my partner and I established M&M Meat Shops. We set up a single retail outlet (about 1,000 square feet) to sell flash frozen foods. It was on Victoria Street South in Kitchener, Ontario. Just 9 months later, at the request of a friend, we opened our first franchised outlet. It was in Cambridge, Ontario.

We proceeded to open 2 to 3 franchised stores each year for our first 5 years of operation. During this time, we were increasingly drawn away from the over-the-counter sales work in our corporate store and into the office doing franchise-related work.

We found ourselves:

- helping new franchisees execute leases in strip plazas;

- negotiating franchise agreements;

- working with food suppliers to negotiate the best 'buys' for our franchisees;

- planning marketing activities for the franchisees;

- assisting franchisees in the staff training process;

- developing an operations manual;

....and the list goes on and on.

We came to rely on our corporate store staff to manage the day-to-day operation of the business. Almost unknowingly, we were fully immersed in the franchise business, which was a totally different business from retail frozen food sales.

Let's go back to the 'dual nature of franchising.' With the knowledge of the very high level of both business and people management skills required to build a franchise company, entrepreneurs can determine the future direction of the company. If they believe that the leadership of the franchise business should be in the hands of experienced management personnel, a lesser role in the franchise business is still an option. Entrepreneurs must focus on their personal strengths and realize that they simply cannot be all things to all people. Maybe the entrepreneur would become positioned as the chief buyer, or in real estate site selection, or in finances, or especially store operations.

There are certainly a wide variety of opportunities for the entrepreneur/prospective franchisor in establishing the franchise structure. These key decisions made by the entrepreneur, prior to franchising, will determine the ultimate level of success of the franchise business! And they're not easy decisions to make early on.

*A franchisor is in two businesses, and successful franchisors are successful in both.*

# Is Your Business Franchisable?

A franchise will only work if it is the right business. In my view, seven basic factors must be present for a business to grow into a successful franchise:

## A. *The market must accept the product or service.*

There must be a demand in the marketplace for the product or service. It cannot satisfy only a small niche in a very specific territory, and the concept must be more than a fad. It must be an established trend, supported by proven long-term sales.

## B. *A successful prototype must exist.*

This prototype is often the owner's original business and becomes the model business or store upon which others are based. This unit must be operated until all problems are removed and it is running smoothly, efficiently and profitably. Strong prototypes are critical for several reasons:

- they help award the business concept to potential franchisees;
- they allow franchisors to make mistakes and refine the concept before franchising additional units;
- they often act as a training ground for future franchisees.

## C. *The training time period must be appropriate.*

If the training period is too short, the franchisee will not be ready to enjoy the potential of the franchise. On the other hand, if the training is too long, it could pose considerable financial hardship on the prospective franchisee because of the franchisee's lack of salary during this period. It's possible that a business is not a franchisable because the training period cannot be established within a reasonable length of time.

*D. The franchisor must be able to detail every aspect of the business.*

Comprehensive manuals (e.g. operations, training and computer manuals) help achieve the standardization required. Uniformity and standardization are critical to build an easily identifiable image. In retail, for example, customers must receive what they expect, regardless of which store they enter.

*E. The partnership between franchisor and franchisee must be mutually beneficial.*

The franchisee benefits from training, guidance and advice provided by the franchisor. The franchisor benefits from the growth of the business and additional revenues that the franchisees fuel. The franchisor can concentrate on the growth potential, service/operations concept, delivery system, image of the franchise and research and development.

*F. A successful franchise must have a proper control mechanism.*

The franchisor's concept must be duplicated in every store. Control is maintained by developing rigid operating specifications, proper franchise management and employee training. Every operational detail in every franchised business must be documented and monitored. Exact duplication establishes the brand, and the brand is strong when consumers know exactly what to expect – no surprises.

*G. The franchisor must be able to consistently distribute the goods or services to the franchisee at a reasonable cost and on a timely basis.*

In its simplest definition, franchising is a marketing and distribution system. There are opportunities for franchising in retail, service, manufacturing and wholesale. Once understood, franchising can be applied to almost any market, industry, product or service. Franchisors who believe that the franchisees are their strategic business partners and who are committed to making them successful at all costs will create for themselves a very profitable business.

## THE METHODS OF FRANCHISING

The most common method of franchising involves single unit franchises, whereby the franchisee is granted the right to operate a single outlet or franchise, often at a predetermined geographic location. It remains the prevalent form of franchising because it offers the advantage of having the franchisee owner remain as the operator. The owner/operator is often recognized as one of the most beneficial aspects of franchising one's business, as unlike an employee, the operator has a uniquely vested interest in the outlet's performance.

Beyond single unit franchising, many franchisors will offer multi-area development agreements to strong franchisee candidates. As part of the contract, the franchisee must open a number of stores in a specific territory in a set period of time. The advantage to the franchisee is that they know they have a secured territory. The franchisor must be careful not to award large territories unless the franchisee has a proven track record.

Also common in many franchise companies are master licensing or sub-franchising arrangements. The franchisor grants a license to a company or person for a territory. The company or person that develops the territory sub-licenses the franchisees according to the franchisor's specifications. This method of expansion allows the company to accelerate its growth but has the disadvantage to the franchisor in that there is a certain loss of direct control over standards and procedures.

Generally speaking any method beyond single unit growth is seen as more advanced, and left for a later stage of development.

## Should I Franchise?

Typically, an entrepreneur establishes a business with one or several company owned outlets and then asks the big question – "Should I franchise my business?" Obviously it's a question that should generate considerable discussion before a final decision is made. Prospective franchisors have to understand that they will change the entire business strategy by entering the world of franchising.

To franchise the business is to set up a system to "clone" all of the methodologies and prescribed specifications of operating the business. In other words, can the ideas and concepts that made the company successful be structured, systemized, recorded and so disciplined that they can be duplicated in a franchise format.

Very often, the initial considerations for franchising are triggered by friends or business associates who express a desire to set up a business identical to that of the first outlet in another location or community. This is usually a good indication that perhaps the business is expandable. It has often been written that a business is franchisable if there is a demand to replicate it. This is certainly an obvious prerequisite to franchising, but the business also needs to make sound financial sense for both franchisor and franchisee. The franchisee must not only have the ability to earn a reasonable rate of return on the investment, but also to be able to afford to pay reasonable royalty fees to the franchisor. The franchisee business can only expand and prosper if sufficient royalty fees are paid to allow the franchisor to provide the support services to the franchisee.

The initial franchise fee generally goes to establishing the franchised business. Most franchisors don't expect any significant profits from the franchise fee. This fee goes towards the franchisor's expenses in connection with attracting and screening the right candidates, site selection, legal, etc. It also covers the initial marketing of the franchise, training and supporting the franchisee prior to and at opening, etc.

Any franchised company that depends on the franchise fee as its primary source of revenue is doomed to failure. Franchised companies need to depend on a regular royalty fee to survive and prosper.

Royalty fees are paid for revenue generated in the prior reporting period because:

- the support services provided by the franchisor helped the franchisees acquire and develop their ability to use the brand name and operating system to get and keep customers;

- the operating system got the customer to come back; and

- using the franchisor's brand name created a customer;

The ongoing royalty fees must be high enough to allow the franchisor to put the infrastructure in place to support the franchisees and cover miscalculations/mistakes along the way. On the other hand, it cannot be so high that it leaves little on the bottom line for the franchisees.

So even before the first franchise is licensed, the prospective franchisor must analyze and re-analyze the financial composition of the business in order to establish the appropriate royalty fee.

Can the franchise fee and royalty fees be changed as the company grows? Most franchise companies will increase the franchise fee as demand for the franchise increases and as the up-front support services expand. However, most successful franchise companies have a standard franchise agreement and one royalty fee for every franchisee in the chain. Uniformity, conformity and fairness in all aspects of the franchise business normally lead to franchisee contentment.

In the early years of development of the franchise, the franchisor is obviously very keen to license operators. There is little or no brand awareness and so franchisors are really asking others to buy into their dream. In exchange, the franchisor typically offers a large, protected territory, or a long-term franchise agreement with many renewals, or other inducements to making the deal. However, as the company grows, the franchisor must establish consistency in all aspects of the franchise agreement, especially on renewals of the agreement. The franchisor can't make special concessions for individual franchisees and expect that they will remain confidential. Interestingly, at M&M Meat Shops, we've come to understand that franchisees simply want the same deal as everyone else. Yes, there will always be those who want special concessions, but when we explain that we treat everyone the same, they appreciate our desire for fairness in all dealings. Remembering that many franchisees are putting their life savings on the line, the last thing they want to discover is that they didn't make the best deal possible when they signed up. Hence, franchise agreements should be carefully crafted, by a franchise lawyer preferably, and then should be non-negotiable.

## THE BENEFITS AND DRAWBACKS OF FRANCHISING

The primary reason for franchising is to achieve faster growth by allowing other people's money to finance the majority of the expansion.

Franchising is a business strategy used to quickly and successfully penetrate, develop, dominate and achieve a strong share of a market.

Here's a short list of some of the advantages and disadvantages to franchising.

### A. Advantages

#### (i) Rapid Growth

A major advantage of franchising is the high rate of growth that can be achieved by accessing franchisees' financial resources. Independent (non-franchised) businesses must finance growth through debt, equity or internally generated funds. And, of course, there is a limit to the amount of debt a bank will support. Growth is very important to businesses, particularly those that do not have ownership of a unique process (such as through a patent). These organizations must compete by outflanking the competition – i.e. locking up good sites, staff and loyal customers.

#### (ii) Committed Labour

Franchisees are more determined than employees to make the business successful because they have a financial stake in the business. They generally have more confidence and ability, and they have a deep concern for their employees and customers. This level of commitment is often very difficult to find in a managerial employee, especially during rapid expansion.

## *(iii) Personal Satisfaction*

Franchisors award franchises for their own personal satisfaction. It becomes a positive reflection on the franchisor's business abilities. So, there is tremendous personal satisfaction by providing others with the opportunity for success and financial rewards. And franchisees get personal satisfaction from owning the assets and operating their own business. Consequently, franchisees share pride with the franchisor as the organization grows.

## *(iv) Pooling Ideas*

As the company grows, there are a growing number of franchisees with similar goals. They all deal in different markets and encounter various unique situations throughout the course of business, each coming up with creative solutions to these problems. By setting up a system to transfer information (i.e. Manuals, Advisory and Marketing Councils, Operations or Renovations Committees, etc.) throughout the chain and capitalizing on this resource, the entire franchise concept will continuously improve and strengthen, benefiting both franchisor and franchisees.

## *(v) Sharing Risk*

By franchising individual units, the franchisor is able to share financial and human resource risks with the franchisee, who in turn accepts most expenses involved. If the store closes, the franchisor may well be liable to certain creditors. Many franchisors will lease the premises and then sub-lease them to the franchisee. This is called a

"Head" lease. It is done in order that the franchisor may maintain control of the site. So, in these situations, if the franchisee defaults, the landlord turns to the franchisor for lease payments. Also, there could be liability to suppliers who were guaranteed payment by the franchisor.

### (vi) Extensive Advertising

Advertising is critical to the success of any business, but it's expensive. The pooled advertising funds from the franchisees provides for a widespread, comprehensive advertising campaign that aids in the growth of existing outlets and warrants the formation of new ones. The added exposure of a large network of franchisees gives the organization greater credibility and power with consumers and suppliers.

### (vii) Purchasing Power

The franchisor establishes a central purchasing department, which in turn secures price reductions on supplies and services. This collective buying power dramatically affects the franchisee's profitability.

### (viii) Reduction of Costly Duplication

The franchisor acts as a central administrative centre, thereby standardizing and reducing the franchisees' administrative functions. Central accounting, purchasing, training and marketing departments relieve the franchisees of responsibilities, allowing them to concentrate on daily operations. Alternatively, relieving the franchisor of day-to-day operational responsibilities means that head office can be run with significantly fewer employees.

## B. *Disadvantages Or Risks*

Although there are a great number of benefits to franchising, there are some disadvantages or risks to this business format:

### (i) *Regulation and Documentation*

Because of the complex nature of franchising, franchisors and other legal advisors must prepare comprehensive franchise agreements, training and operations manuals, etc. Franchisors in Canada are increasingly being asked to disclose financial statements, copies of all agreements to be signed by the franchisees, and information about the background of the franchisor's principals. The cost and time involved in preparing all this documentation is significant.

### (ii) *Potential Litigation*

Franchisees invest considerable monies in the franchise and sign comprehensive legal agreements. Lawsuits can arise when the franchisee feels that they have been treated unfairly, or if either party feels that the other has broken one of the promises in the agreement.

### (iii) *Decreased Control*

Although both the franchisor and franchisee have signed a franchise agreement, it is not always easy to enforce, regulate and otherwise control every single aspect of the business. The head office in a non-franchised business, by contrast, can simply dictate to the unit managers. The franchisor cannot simply dismiss the franchisee as they are not employees. In fact, because of the complex legal nature of the business, and the fact that the franchisee has typically made a significant investment, franchisees usually need to be convinced that a change is a good one, before it will be accepted.

### (iv) Long Term Relationship

Frequently, over time, franchisees feel that they have learned the business in-depth and in turn may want operational independence from the franchisor. Obviously, this is very frustrating for the franchisor. The franchisor faces a constant challenge to change and upgrade the concept and product line to keep the franchisees content. The franchise relationship requires a long-term commitment from both parties and ongoing leadership by the franchisor.

### (v) Sharing Profits

In a franchised organization, the franchisor makes less profit per unit because the franchisee has accepted responsibility for the success of the unit. The franchisee bears much of the investment burden and hence is entitled to most of the profits. The franchisor's return on investment is usually less than if the units are corporately owned.

# CHAPTER 2

*Rajiv Mathur*
*Deloitte & Touche LLP*

*Bob Bougie*
*Deloitte & Touche LLP*

## THE FINANCIAL ASPECTS OF BECOMING A FRANCHISOR

Whether you are a budding entrepreneur with a franchising glimmer in your eye, a large business with a number of outlets and expansion plans in the wings, a businessperson who wants to convert existing units into franchises, or a franchisor with one or two successful outlets, the economics of franchising will be of keen interest to you. This chapter discusses the financial aspects of being a franchisor, and includes information for franchise area developers, or those who hold a master franchise or sub-franchise.

In particular, it will discuss:

- The economics of successful franchising

- How to prepare the financial model you will need

- The real costs of becoming a franchisor

- The returns – for franchisor and franchisee

- How to finance system growth

- Bank financing and bank franchise programs

- Government financial assistance

- Financial information systems – reporting and control

- Troubleshooting strategies to avert failure

## THE ECONOMICS OF SUCCESSFUL FRANCHISING

### A. *The Financial Upside*

As an alternative to franchising, businesses seeking to expand would have to obtain financing from internally generated funds and/or outside capital by borrowing or by selling equity. Both these forms of capital can be difficult to obtain or unduly expensive, especially for businesses in early stages of growth. Franchising can provide you with an alternative approach. You can enjoy:

- Accessible financing, using franchisee equity and debt capacity. Although you must pay the cost of creating a franchise program, your franchisees will bear the remaining costs of expansion and much of the risk as well. Franchisees typically invest their own money and operate the franchise they have purchased themselves.

- An immediate source of revenue. Franchisees usually pay the franchisor an up-front franchise fee, plus ongoing royalties.

- Return on goodwill. Franchising can eventually transform intangible goodwill in your business into income from franchise sales.

- An extremely motivated workforce. A franchised business can potentially grow more quickly – and make you more money – than a non-franchised business. That is mostly because if you choose carefully, undermotivated franchisees or unenthusiastic dealers are the exception, not the rule. They can bring in unencumbered money, which enables you to raise more funds. They will be managing their shop under your structured guidelines. You can control their expansion carefully. And hard-working owner-operators – at least the vast majority of them – are motivated to make money.

- Better unit-level performance. When franchised, the profitability of marginal units or stores increases.

- Fewer hassles. You give up the burdens and costs of payroll, funding employee benefits, absenteeism, theft, and other problems associated with operating a business on a day-to-day basis.

- Buying power. As the franchise expands, it and corporate-owned outlets are eligible for better buying opportunities.

- A more marketable business. A rapidly growing and profitable franchise system can be a more salable commodity than a conventional business.

## B. The Risks

Before you pop any champagne bottles, it is important to keep in mind that franchising is not risk-free. Most notably:

- You might not select the right franchisees. Getting rid of a bad franchisee is much more difficult than getting rid of a bad employee.

- If you already operate a successful business, your time and energy away from it and spent on franchise system development may mean reduced earnings and impaired cash flow.

- Most franchise systems do not become profitable until a number of units are operating successfully. You may have to rely on your flagship business to provide you with working capital.

- Novice franchisees who may not yet be effective could damage your business while using your trademarks, name and style of business. Disgruntled customers do not differentiate between you and your franchisees.

## C. The Building Blocks Of Financial Success

Every business success story is unique. Nonetheless, successful new franchisors have more in common than you might guess. They share:

- A sound financial strategy. A weak financial structure will endanger your business from within more than any other single factor. A strong strategy is your best defense against the threats and pressures related to system start-up or conversion. An important component of this strategy is proper financing for both you and your franchisees. No matter how smart you are or how good your product or service is, if you are not properly financed you are going to fail.

- Financial discipline. An understanding of finance basics is critical. Do you know how to read income statements and balance sheets and manage cash flow? Do your franchisees? Does your cash come in every 30, 60, 90 or 120 days? Have you ensured your franchise fee, royalties and other fees from franchisees match up with your outflow (payments to suppliers)? You will have to know exactly how to set your costs against your financial recoveries, item by item.

- An understanding of the other disciplines of franchising. Successful franchisors must also be knowledgeable about – and understand the financial implications of – operations, marketing, advertising, legal, sales, financial, organizational and human resources. A breakdown in any one of these disciplines could result in a breakdown in the entire system.

- The ability to build franchise value. You create value for franchisees by building your brand name, products, services and support. Your customers will demonstrate their appreciation for these efforts through repeat business.

- Hands-on franchisees. Franchisees who are active and committed owner-operators build value and wealth for themselves and their franchisors. They recognize the value of being part of the franchise system, so they do not resent paying royalties.

- A win-win situation for both franchisee and franchisor. Both franchisees and franchisors have to make an acceptable return on their respective investments. This means that if you are operating a business with certain profit today, you should only think of franchising once you can show your franchisees how to make a reasonable return, and leave some for you, based on your respective expectations. Ultimately, your goals should be to build, teach and train franchisees, so they can pay you and help you sell more franchises.

## PREPARING YOUR FINANCIAL MODEL

### A. First, Develop The Right Framework

It is important to determine your business situation first, then develop a financial model that meets its requirements. This financial model – and the framework around which you build it – should be an accurate reflection of your business case.

### (i) Choosing your development path

To begin with, you need to choose between two different development paths: product/service franchising or business format franchising.

Product/service franchising. Here, you license franchisees to sell or distribute goods or services using your trademark. They are otherwise free to conduct business as they see fit. If you opt for this development path, you need to further choose:

- A licensing arrangement. The licensor grants the licensee the right to use patents, know-how or trademarks. A license fee often applies.

- Distributorship. A manufacturer sells his or her product exclusively to the distributor at wholesale prices. The distributor can resell those products, and does not have to pay the manufacturer royalties on gross sales.

- Dealership. The dealer buys products at wholesale prices and resells directly to consumers, but is not usually restricted to selling one manufacturer's products.

Business format franchising. In contrast, this involves franchising a complete business method, from site development to operating methods. Because it demands considerably more organizational and financial resources from franchisors than product or service franchising, many franchise systems, such as fast food chains, include aspects of both business format and product franchising.

## *(ii) Selecting the right method*

Beyond your development path, you need to select the franchise method that will work best for you, taking the advantages, disadvantages, income and costs into consideration. The following methods are most common:

- Single-unit franchising. Franchisees invest their own capital in exchange for the right to operate the franchised business at a specified location.

- Multiple-unit franchising. A franchisor grants a franchisee the right to open a set number of units (often called an "area developer"), and/or the right to grant subfranchises (often called a "master franchise"). In many cases, this type of growth comes at a later stage of development of a franchise system.

- Turnkey and semi-turnkey franchising. In a turnkey operation, the franchisor is responsible for selecting, acquiring, developing and stocking the location. For semi-turnkey operations, the franchisee shares some of these activities with the franchisor. In addition to franchise fees, franchisees pay the franchisor the costs of establishing the franchised business, often with a mark-up, as a development fee.

- Conversion franchising. Here, the franchisor can offer independent operators the opportunity to become part of an existing franchise system, such as a real estate business or a chain of travel agencies, which are already related to the franchisor's business. Because sites are already operating, the costs of establishing the business are greatly reduced.

- Co-branding. This is a combination of two – or more – businesses operating in one location, for example, a coffee and donut franchise in a service station. The smaller business piggybacking onto the large one reduces its start-up costs and risks, and increases its start-up cash flow. The larger business benefits from reduced labour and occupancy costs. Both businesses benefit in terms of customer traffic and real estate costs.

## B. Doing Your Homework

A solid financial plan requires a lot of preparatory work. Consider the following three "assignments", as a means of reviewing whether you have done enough homework to start franchising.

### (i) Assignment #1:

*Learn the importance of a good business plan*

Whether or not you need outside financing, preparing a formal business plan before you consider franchising is a worthwhile activity, because it forces you to think through all aspects of your business and to create a roadmap showing where you want to go, how you will get there, and how your franchising plans fit in.

Outside financiers will carefully scrutinize your business plan's financial section, which should include financial statements, financial forecasts (balance sheet, income statement and cash flow) and financing and capitalization requirements. They will be particularly interested in the evidence you can provide that your business plan will work for both your franchisees and for you.

---

*Preparing a formal business plan before you consider franchising is a worthwhile activity, because it forces you to think through all aspects of your business and to create a roadmap*

---

## (ii) Assignment #2:

*Determine whether your idea will really work for the franchisees*

As a franchisor, your customers are your franchisees. In a sense, you should think of them as business partners. You can keep them happy by providing them with the product and support they need to make a reasonable living and a competitive return on their investment.

The franchise business needs higher than average profitability to generate enough to share between franchisee and franchisor, allowing for a reasonable management salary. Given that royalties are typically 4% to 10% of gross sales and advertising an additional 2%, if you cannot see at least 20% profit in your core business investment, franchising may not be viable for you.

A franchisee's return on investment should also be somewhat greater than average – say 20% – with the possible potential for further growth potential.

To ensure that this business provides a reasonable living for a franchisee, it's also important to analyze whether the time it will take your franchisee to pay back the initial investment to you and/or financial institutions is reasonable.

---

*As a franchisor, your customers are your franchisees....
You can keep them happy by providing
them with the product and support they
need to make a reasonable living*

---

You can begin to determine the financial viability of your potential franchisees by developing realistic financial statements, including income statements and cash flow projections. If you have one or more existing locations, you can use your actual results and existing financial statements as a starting point. The longer your existing locations have been in operation, the more reliable your analysis will be. Two or three years of actual experience of operating a typical unit is better than pages of assumptions.

Here are a few other suggestions to help you determine whether this idea will work for you as well as franchisees:

- Evaluate the effect on initial franchise investment of different business unit models. This may suggest a change in architecture, interior design or equipment.

- Estimate the initial cost of the franchise comprised of the initial franchise fee, goodwill and other hard costs of a turnkey business operation. A franchisee's total investment can vary tremendously, depending on how well established the franchise is as well as its business format and size.

- For each potential franchisee location, develop sales projections that take into account local competition and demographics and sales performance of other similar existing locations.

- Consider different sales scenarios (conservative and optimistic), different mixes of products and services, changes in store hours, changes to staffing, sources of supply, a sensitivity analysis which takes into consideration potential highs and lows, and any other possibilities that may change operating results.

- Identify all fees the franchisee will pay. Many of these will depend on the franchising approach you have chosen, but they should also include royalties, advertising, training, and product margin, etc.

- Prepare franchisee income and expenses statements using the fees you have identified. Franchisee operating expenses should include all the usual items in an income statement, such as wages, occupancy, insurance, utilities, and so on.

- Compute franchisee earnings after considering financing costs. The initial investment may be assumed to be funded by debt and equity, say 2/3 debt and 1/3 equity. Then reduce the after-tax earnings by the loan payments to determine the free cash flow accruing to the franchisee.

*(iii)Assignment #3:*

*Determine whether it will work for the franchisor*

It is also important to conduct your own financial planning to see if franchising will work for you. Before you can even begin to project your income and expenses, you need to take several important realities into consideration.

- The number and speed of new units: Your projected income will likely be driven by how quickly you can open new franchised units and the total number of units you have in operation. Each new unit brings franchise fee income and has associated costs. The increasing cumulative total number of units determines your royalty income.

- Your balance of franchised and corporate units: Your projected income statement also depends on how many units are going to be opened as – or converted to – franchises. If you have one existing unit, you may not want to franchise it right away and instead keep it as a corporate store. One or more corporate units can be used for training new franchisees and for trying out new products and procedures.

- Your timelines for success: Your cash flow, when graphed against time, will probably look like a kind of "bathtub curve." The time required to get through the trough is usually not as fast as you'd like. Typically, a new franchise system begins its financial reality with a starting cash position while it builds its infrastructure. While the franchisor busily develops its systems, but before any new units are sold, all costs represent negative cash flow. This is one end of the bathtub. Then, as new franchise units are opened, income from franchise fees and royalties balance out against ongoing costs. The bathtub begins to flatten out. If your financial plan is on target, cash flow may become positive somewhere between the 24th and 36th month from inception. From that point forward, income exceeds expenses and the system generates a profit. Once profits accumulate and the original investment is recaptured, you are in a positive cash flow position – typically between the third and fifth years for a new franchise system.

• The need to keep the model current: Many successful franchisors use the five-year financial model just described to plan growth. They also take the time to carry out an annual planning exercise during which they reconcile the model to reality, adjust existing forecast openings, and extend plans into the fifth year. Each year, plan to explore at least two financial possibilities: one conservative, the other aggressive in terms of growth. Look at worst-case scenarios for each plan with respect to expenses and revenues.

• Start-up considerations: The early stages of franchise system development require time and energy for planning. This is no problem for companies with staff available to perform the planning task, but if you are an owner-operator you may well need to devote your time and energy to operating the business. At the same time, you still have to rely on it – or your flagship store – to support you and provide working capital during franchise system start-up.

- Balance income against costs: In the early stages of the franchise system development, most of your franchise income will come from the sale of new franchised units. But if your financial modelling relies heavily upon these fees, you will be too busy selling new franchises as opposed to supporting your existing franchisees. While the sale of new units provides a source of income to cover your startup costs, over time, it is imperative that income from ongoing fees – like royalties and markups on inventory – adequately covers ongoing costs.

- Capital requirements: The key to successful franchising, like in all businesses, is not to be undercapitalized. You need to forecast how much cash you need to start the franchise system development and to sustain it during the early years, until it reaches the break-even point. Use your income statement projections and projected cash flow to prepare a monthly analysis to the end of the year of your anticipated break-even point, then an annual analysis through to the fifth year.

## THE REAL COSTS OF BECOMING A FRANCHISOR

In the previous section of this chapter, you've learned about the importance of overall financial planning and of carefully developing the right financial framework for you. It's particularly important to take the time to plan and assess your costs before you begin building a franchise system.

You are now ready to figure out how much this franchising venture will really set you back. There are a number of costs you will need to include in your analysis and income projections:

## A. *Franchisor's Start-up and Operating Costs*

During early stages, costs are typically high and revenues low. Costs will include some or all of the following services:

(i)   A marketing program. This is your program to convince potential franchisees you have the best product, service and franchise system in the world. You will likely have to pay for the following components of a marketing program:

- Franchise package: promotional literature, audio-visual material, website, financial information

- Salespeople's salaries

- Travel and entertainment related to selling franchises.

(ii)  Training program and operating manual. Both initial and ongoing training are critical to ensure franchisees provide quality products and services that conform to the franchisor's standards. Franchisor costs related to a training program include:

- development of operating manual

- trainers' salaries

- development and revision of training materials

- franchisee and staff orientation

- training at head-office, at other franchisee locations, or outside training.

(iii) Accounting program. A franchisor must establish its own accounting policies and procedures, as well as a program for franchisees. This may include:

- writing policies and procedures

- developing an accounting manual

- consider performing certain accounting functions, depending on your ability

- selecting appropriate accounting software and/or point of sale systems for use at franchisee locations.

(iv) Printing costs. At franchise system start-up, you will need to print copies of a variety of documents including:

- training and operating manuals

- accounting manuals and reporting forms

- disclosure document

- franchise package materials

- franchisee applications, franchise agreements.

(v) Head Office. At the outset it is often the case that revenue from franchising may not justify the expense of maintaining a separate head office. However, invariably as franchise systems grow, a head office and its costs will be a necessity.

(vi) Professional services. Most franchise system start-up requirements demand professional services requiring outside personnel that even large franchisors, and certainly smaller or owner-operated companies, do not have on staff:

- Consulting services. In many cases a prospective franchisor should seriously consider conducting an independent analysis to establish whether the business concept can be franchised. There is also merit in getting independent verification of work already done by the franchisor. Other consulting services may include:
  - market research
  - strategic planning and business planning
  - development of any or all of the components of the marketing package, for example, websites, videos and brochure text
  - franchise sales
  - implementation programs, franchisee relations programs, field operations
  - programs
  - site selection
  - negotiation of loans
  - franchise program re-engineering.
- Legal services. At the beginning of the franchise system development, you will need legal services to:
  - draft franchise agreements
  - prepare disclosure documents – required by law in Alberta, Ontario and the United States.
  - register trademarks, service marks and logos
  - international licensing

- draft letters of intent

- lease/sublease arrangements.

- Accounting services. You may require an accounting firm to:

  - prepare or review your financial plans

  - advise you on tax implications of your plan, and to develop a tax plan

  - help you develop a method to monitor and control franchisees.

- Advertising. You may need creative work to develop a logo and other elements of a standardized corporate image or "look." throughout the system:

Other costs associated with advertising include:

  - developing an advertising program

  - placing ads in a variety of media.

- Site selection, real estate services, construction supervision. The cost of professional services to help find, lease, buy, build or renovate franchise locations could include:

  - real estate services

  - construction and/or supervision of construction projects

  - travel expenses to and from potential locations.

## B. Development Costs

Plugging the costs of adding new franchisees into your financial model will help you calculate the number of new units you will need to reach the break-even point. These include:

- Organizational costs. As your franchise system grows, you will need additional personnel in all the key areas of the business including marketing, field staff, training, etc.

- Location costs. Depending on your franchising method, you may incur site location, lease/purchase and development costs. Locations in busy shopping malls in particular are difficult to acquire and sometimes costly.

- Special deals. Early in your franchise program, you may decide to respond to franchisees seeking, or demanding, special deals ranging from discounts on franchise fees to subsidized rent. You may choose to comply with these requests to spur business, but remember to plug the numbers into your financial model.

- Franchise advertising and grand opening.

- Franchisee recruiting. Finding and evaluating prospective franchisees can be costly. You need to interview, prepare a detailed information package, check references, perform credit checks, and so on.

- Franchisee training. This is an important and necessary expense.

## THE RETURNS – FOR FRANCHISOR AND FRANCHISEE

Only adequate returns for both franchisor and franchisee will ensure the success of your business venture.

### A. *Franchisor Returns and Sources of Income*

Your financial planning should take all possible sources of income into consideration, and also set out strategies for income streams in the future. You will not be able to realize all or even many of the potential income alternatives set out in this chapter, but you may discover a possibility or two.

In any case, it is important to cautiously structure your business model to control your sources of income. Initiating a variety of potential income sources to your franchisee does not necessarily increase the amount of income flowing to you. Many potential income sources may instead add to the management complexity and necessitate added controls over responsibilities, obligations and even risks – without necessarily increasing your bottom line.

It is also important – and in some cases legally required – that you disclose to prospective franchisees all expected sources of income and whether they are based on cost recovery or for profit.

The different sources of franchisor revenue include:

### (i) *Franchise fee*

A franchise fee is paid by the franchisee in exchange for the right to operate a franchised unit using the franchisor's systems and name. Franchisors use this fee to cover all costs related to establishing the franchisee and the location, including return on goodwill. How much to charge? Certainly franchisors with smaller recruitment costs may profit significantly. Franchisors whose system is in high demand may increase franchise fees and profit from the increase. Competition will have an impact on determining your franchise fee. In general, though, franchise fees should cover the franchisor's recruitment costs, training, return on goodwill, and infrastructure investment.

### (ii) Royalties as a percentage of gross sales

Royalties paid on franchisees' retail sales are the income mainstay for most franchisors because this payment method establishes a direct understanding between franchisee and franchisor, and adds credibility to a franchisor's financial model. They should provide you with ongoing returns generated as your franchisees run the operations. In general, royalty percentages are in the range of 4% to 8%, but you will need to determine how much to charge based on your income requirements and what the competition is charging. Small changes in percentages or forms of payment can make a significant difference. Franchisors can increase cash flow, for instance, by requiring weekly instead of monthly payments, and arranging for automatic bank deposits. Some modifications of the basic royalty method include:

- Setting a minimum royalty payment based on the greater of a fixed amount or specified percentage.

- Setting a lower royalty percentage in the early stages of your franchise system development as an enticement to potential franchisees.

### *(iii) Fixed fee royalties*

This is a fixed monthly fee, usually based on specified criteria. With franchised hotels, for instance, the number of rooms may determine the fee.

### *(iv) Equipment sales or leasing, security deposits*

Some franchisors buy equipment and then sell or lease it to franchisees at a rate higher than the purchase price but lower than the franchisees would have paid to purchase or lease for themselves. In addition to the profit on the equipment sale or leasing cost, franchisors can use a pool of deposits as a fund for investment or working capital. It is wise to require a security deposit on this leased equipment, and disclose this practice as a source of profit.

### *(v) Advertising*

In addition to using suppliers' co-op advertising money, most franchisors collect an advertising fee from franchisees as a percentage of gross sales, usually 2% to 3%. It is not normally considered a profit centre and should be accountable to the franchisees annually.

### *(vi) Periodic fees*

A franchisor can set out in the franchise agreement the ability to charge back periodic or regular expenses to franchisees, at cost or for profit. The agreement should spell out these fees, which may include:

- A renewal fee and/or adjustments of other fees to current rates when the franchise agreement is renewed

- A transfer fee to ensure that the franchisor is not out-of-pocket should there be a transfer or resale

- Recovering costs of store upgrading or renovation, at time of renewal or as prescribed in franchise agreement

- Supplemental training, seminars, conventions, refresher courses

## (vii) *Termination, death or disability*

Terminating franchisees can be costly. Franchisors can attempt to limit exposure by stating in the franchise agreement that the franchisee is responsible for costs incurred by the franchisor as a result of a termination by the franchisor. It is important to get a lawyer to review the agreement and ensure that this provision will be enforceable by law.

## (viii) *Interest payments on late payments*

Your franchise agreement should state that interest is payable at a specified rate on late payments and amounts discovered (in an audit) to be in arrears, where the franchisee is at fault. It is wiser to cross-reference these arrears to other agreements or documents than to spell out specific penalties.

## (ix) *Specified services*

The franchisor may supply services to their franchisees. Specified services can include:

- Signage leases. Some franchisors arrange for the leasing of exterior or bulkhead signs to franchisees.

- Bookkeeping and accounting. Franchisors sometimes provide these services to their franchisees. In addition, inspection and audit is usually a cost of doing business, but if an understatement is disclosed, the franchisee usually pays the cost.

- Additional training

- Administration of insurance programs and benefits plans

- Telephone listings

- Computing services

- Construction supervision, architectural services, remodeling

## B. Franchisee Returns and Sources of Income

As we have pointed out earlier, your franchisees are your customers. They are entitled to achieve satisfactory benefits and returns in exchange for the services you provide.

### (i) Franchisee financial returns

Financially, franchisees reap what they sow. Hardworking and committed franchisees in a good location, working within a strong franchise system, can expect to enjoy:

- a reasonable living

- a growth rate greater than rate of inflation

- a strong return on their investment
- the opportunity to build equity

You can calculate franchisees' returns on investment in terms of accumulated profits as a percentage of franchisee's total investment or in terms of the return on investment period – the time it takes for franchisees to earn back their total investment. A reasonable break-even period is usually three to five years, depending on the franchise system's size, total investment and the franchisee's hard work. In great locations, the break-even period can be as short as 18 months.

## (ii) Franchisee non-monetary benefits

If franchisees truly wanted to be independent businesspeople, they would have bought an existing business or started their own. They approach franchisors because they want the benefits of affiliation and are willing to give up some independence in return. Franchisee benefits may include:

- lower risk of failure than independent business
- established product or service
- advertising and marketing support
- franchise identity including name, name recognition, logo, public acceptance
- efficiency in a proven system of operation
- training
- start-up assistance

- franchisee association or advisory committee

- periodic improvements to the franchise system

- group purchasing power through centralized buying

- site selection and development

- accounting assistance, often including a specified accounting system

- assistance in financing

- management and decision-making experience and expertise.

## (iii) The bottom line

Once you have done your financial planning, constructed projected income statements and developed cash flow projections, ask yourself:

- Do these financial results work for me, while still maintaining a reasonable living for the franchisees?

- Is my break-even point between years three and five? If it is before year three, does my plan call for an unrealistically aggressive opening schedule?

- What is this business' rate of return? Is it high enough to make this effort worthwhile? Is it high enough to secure outside financing?

# How to Finance System Growth

Like any business, franchising has a life cycle – from idea, through start-up and growth, to stabilization. You will need different methods to finance the transitions from the early stages of franchise system development up to and including the growth phase.

For new franchisors, getting the funding you need to finance growth is a major hurdle. Unlike many other factors, this one is not entirely under your control. You have to persuade someone else to lend you money or invest in your system, and the decision is his or hers to make. To help you jump this hurdle, this section looks at:

- strategies and attitudes for successful growth
- your financing options for early stages
- financing alternatives for the growth phase, after you have some units running successfully
- how to develop and maintain a successful relationship with your financers.

## A. Strategies and attitudes for successful growth

People choose to franchise because it is an excellent way they can grow an established business without incurring relatively high capital costs. Translate this business philosophy into a positive attitude, and strategies that ensure success will naturally follow.

### (i) Focus on franchise value, not on franchise fees

The correct operating philosophy is 'How can I make my franchise package so valuable that it is a business opportunity in high demand, to be allocated among the most qualified potential franchisees?'

## (ii) Careful early growth lets you finance from within

Most early-stage franchisors are limited in their rate of growth because they are unable to raise sufficient outside capital. If this is your situation, your basic game plan has to be slow and careful growth. You may not be able to afford to go from 10 stores to 15 in one year, but you should intend to grow by one or two at a time.

## (iii) Pace yourself

If you do not control your growth, it will control you and could destroy you. You need to ensure that you have the infrastructure in place before your anticipated growth by setting out a very disciplined growth environment.

Careful pacing is a balancing act. If you hire too many new staffers before many units have been established, for instance, you run the risk of making your organization top heavy. If you sell more units than planned, you may be unexpectedly understaffed. Understand and anticipate changes in resource requirements, so you can plan and react appropriately.

## B. Your Financing Options

Different financing options exist for you, depending upon whether you are at the "glimmer in the eye" stage, the idea launch stage, the start-up stage or the growth phase. Let's take a look at each of these in turn.

## (i) "Glimmer in the eye" stage

Without a proven business model, this is very hard to launch. Generally, the best practice is to have an established business first, then build a franchise model. You need to explore ideas and products, conduct market research and develop your concept. You can get the seed financing you need from:

- personal savings
- first or second mortgage on your property
- enthusiastic friends and family
- an "angel" – private investor, investment company or fund.

## (ii) Idea launch stage

Now it is time to take your plans off the drawing board and put them into action. You are ready to sign a lease, quit your job, purchase equipment, and open a store. If your seed money cannot carry you through, you can look to:

- the bank: you may not qualify for all the funds you need, but you could be eligible for a line of credit, second mortgage or a loan against other assets
- strategic partners: look for a person or company who might benefit economically from your business

## (iii) Start-up stage

Now you are a new franchise system with no pre-existing units, or an existing owner-operated business, with a few units in operation. In addition to the sources of funding listed already, consider also:

- factoring companies: they buy your accounts receivable, pay 70% to 90% immediately, the balance on collection, and charge you a percentage of your monthly sales; they could be particularly suitable if you have a large number of small accounts, though this could be a costly option

- leasing companies, to arrange financing on equipment purchases.

Plus, once you have started operating, you may be able to ask for suppliers / trade credit for extended terms on accounts payable.

## C. Growth Phase

Now you have got a basic infrastructure supporting existing franchised or corporate units, and you are poised to expand. Or you want to renew a stalled franchise program. Or you are a larger company wishing to convert an existing chain into a franchise system. Or you want to invest in a change in your franchise system - you want to introduce new products, for example, expand existing markets or improve your operational performance. Your financing options include:

### (i) Growth from within

Some companies choose to expand only as fast as their existing franchise system can fuel growth. In many cases this is a declared policy, while in other cases the policy is imposed by an inability to find adequate external financing or qualified franchisees.

Advantages: less debt, no loss of equity in exchange for funding, no time and energy spent seeking external financing.

Disadvantage: slower growth.

## (ii) Multi unit franchising

Multiple unit franchising, or growing your franchise through a master-, sub- or area-franchise agreement, is not a form of financing, but its up-front fee can facilitate franchise system growth into a large geographic area. You can stay in control by making sure to include a development schedule that sets out an agreed upon number of units to open per year. You can also ask that your master, sub- or area franchisee demonstrate commitment to your business by ensuring that he or she is not involved in other businesses at the same time.

Advantages: the boost to cash flow can help finance other growth activities and reduce the cost of recruiting and supporting franchisees.

Disadvantages: loss of control; the difficulty of finding the right person to manage the franchisees; putting a time limit on development may result in poor franchise selection; risk of poor performance of franchisee higher with multiple-unit franchise arrangement.

## (iii) Venture capital

You can get venture capital, also called equity financing, in exchange for a share of the business. Usually, a venture capital group wants a say in how you conduct the business, and is willing to arrange for you to buy back your equity at some later time. Venture capital groups are interested in amounts over $250,000, and look for a return on their investment over three to five years – though they usually require a risk premium.

Advantages: venture capital investors can often provide sophisticated financial advice, and your debt is limited to them.

Disadvantage: loss of control; loss of full ownership; the risk that your returns are not sufficient or do not arrive in time to satisfy the venture capitalist.

## (iv) Public offering

Going public, or making an initial public offering, is an important and strategic approach to raising capital. Many factors need to be considered before going public, including:

- the size of your company – for a listing on the Toronto exchange, after-tax earnings must be sufficient to meet their criteria; they can be smaller for other exchanges in Canada

- unique or innovative products or services

- strong management team

- comprehensive business plan

- comprehensive financial reporting systems and procedures

- board of directors with outside directors

- a franchise program with a good track record

- a demonstrably explosive growth operation.

Advantages: can reduce debt, enhanced corporate image, the prospect of offering stock options as incentive.

Disadvantages: management is accountable, you must disclose financial information, administratively time-consuming and costly, rigid regulatory requirements.

### (v) *Private placements / joint ventures*

If your goals match those of a limited group of investors, it might make sense to sell stock or debt to them.

Advantages: often few strings are attached; investors may provide expertise.

Disadvantages: investors may want a say in how the business is run.

### (vi) *Limited partnerships / managing partner plan*

Franchisee-investors can enter into partnership with the franchisor – an attractive arrangement for passive investors who can put up capital but let head office take the lead in running the store.

Advantages: easier to find franchisees because of lower total investment, more streamlined and consistent store-level operations, reduced franchisee/franchisor conflict.

Disadvantages: lower franchise fee means reduced up-front income, franchisee may hire a manager thereby reducing the commitment and hard work of an owner-operator.

### (vii) *Banks and government programs*

This source of financing is so common and so important, especially in Canada, that we have devoted two sections later on in this chapter to them.

## D. *A successful Relationship with Your Financers*

A franchise system is like a three-legged stool, with one leg for the franchisor, another for the franchisees, and the third for your suppliers. More often than not, your bank and other financiers are that third leg. To maintain your balance, you have to create and prepare documents, handle the tough questions and successfully maintain your ongoing relationship.

### (i) *Planning and preparation of documents are keys to obtaining financing*

For most formal sources of funding, you need a business plan that includes a detailed financial plan. Refer back to the beginning of this chapter for suggestions on how to proceed.

### (ii) *Anticipate the hard questions*

Whether you are seeking funds from a bank or another source, plan ahead for your meetings with potential financiers by anticipating their questions:

- Why are you franchising? Is it because you have run into serious problems at corporate locations? To cope with economic pressures? Increased competition?

- Have you completed a franchise feasibility analysis? Does it include: marketing program, supply of product, financial stability, qualified personnel, and ongoing development?

- Do you have a site selection process? Franchisee selection process?

- Have you established a control and monitoring system with clearly identified

early warning signs and the actions you
will take to handle problems? Do you
have a track record in dealing with ailing
and failing franchisees – a particular
challenge for new franchisors, according
to many bankers.

## BANK FINANCING AND BANK FRANCHISE PROGRAMS

In the earlier stages of franchise system development, you
may not be eligible for bank financing, or may obtain only
limited bank financing. But eventually, like most businesses
seeking financing, you will need to head for the bank. Banks are
a good source of short-term working capital for smaller and
mid-sized companies, and an important first contact for any
company in need of capital. They can also be part of a franchise
plan that provides a tailored financing package to franchisees.

### A. Bank Financing

Banks and other conventional financial institutions do not
like to take excessive risks. They prefer loaning money to
businesses with better-than-average chances of success, and are
most comfortable with an experienced entrepreneur, proven
product or established system. While banks do not set out to
reject applications, they are careful who they deal with, because
they are always looking to minimize potential loan losses by
investing only in the best run, best managed franchise systems.

#### (i) Shopping for a bank or financial institution

First and foremost, remember that you can shop
around. Start with chartered banks and trust
companies. Today major chartered banks have
national franchise services and other independent

business centres. If possible, choose a commercial branch rather than a consumer branch. During your selection process, ask:

- Does the institution have branches in all markets you plan to open franchise units?
- What banking services are offered to franchisors? To franchisees?
- What are the lending criteria?
- Do they have franchising specialists on staff?

## (ii) Types of loans

The following types of loans are generally available from banks, but may also be available from other lenders.

- Term loan. You can use a fixed term loan (a loan repayable over a fixed period of time) to purchase assets, expand your business or acquire a business. Terms vary from one to five years, repayable (in other words, amortized) over eight to 15 years. Security is usually in the form of fixed assets. Like any other type of loan, you should match the debt with what you want to finance.

- Mortgages. You can generally borrow up to about 60% of the value of commercial real estate, secured against the property. Terms range from one to five years, and amortization may be from 15 to 25 years.

- Operating loan. These are short-term loans – for one year, maximum – to cover your day-to-day working capital needs for operating expenses. More often than not, they are on a demand basis. They can be in the form of direct demand advances, overdrafts, bankers' acceptances or letters of credit. Operating loans are typically secured with accounts receivable (65% to 85% of receivables under 60 or 90 days) and inventory (40% to 50% of cost on hand).

- Line of credit. This is not a loan per se: it is an agreement between you and your lender that sets the maximum amount you can draw and conditions for repayment.

- Letter of credit. When a franchisor purchases supplies from a foreign manufacturer, your supplier may require payment in the form a letter of credit issued by the bank.

- Bankers' acceptances. These are short-term financing (typically 30 to 365 days) at market-sensitive rates. Acceptances take the form of a draft to be paid on a specified date. Upon acceptance by a chartered bank, the draft is like a certified cheque.

*(iii) Applying for a loan*

Prepare appropriate documents in advance and anticipate the questions you will be asked. Even if you have sufficient personal property to secure a loan, most banks will require a business plan. Use a financial advisor or accountant to help you develop a loan application strategy, draft documents and rehearse for key meetings. If someone else has prepared your business plan, make sure you completely understand it before meeting with your banker. Expect some variation of the following questions:

- Describe your cash flow?
- How long have you been in business?
- Exactly what do you need the money for?
- What is your equity?
- Exactly what is your involvement?

*(iv) Lending criteria*

When evaluating applications, lenders use a formula known as the four Cs.

- Character – What is the character of the businessperson? Have they been bankrupt before? What is this person's reputation in the business community?

- Capacity – Does the business and management have the capacity to turn their business plan into action? Do they have the capacity to repay a loan from future cash flow?

- Conditions – What are the conditions outside the applicant's control that may affect the business? These conditions include interest rates, labour supply, barriers to market entry and competition.

- Collateral – What collateral can the applicant offer as security for the loan? Examples include assets such as inventory, receivables, equipment or buildings, personal guarantees or mortgages on personal property, or another guarantor.

## B. Creating a Franchise Plan for Financing at Your Bank

Most Canadian banks have franchise programs or franchise plans that serve both the franchisor and the franchisee network.

### (i) The franchisor side of a franchise plan

For the franchisor, a customized franchise plan can provide the following services and loans:

- Corporate financing – operating and term loans, leasing, bankers' acceptances and letters of credit

- Cash management – centralized banking, funds-gathering from franchisees, payroll, payment distribution

- Financial information support – cash management, cash flow planning, lease administration

### (ii) The franchisee side of a bank franchise plan

A franchise plan may have a separate franchisee assistance plan which deals with the financial needs of franchisees, such as franchisee financing and other banking services. Once established, this type of financing can ease and quicken the process of getting a new franchisee up and running. An important criterion for franchisee financing – and one usually specified in a franchise plan – is franchisee equity. A franchisor and bank may establish a franchisee financing program, for instance, in which franchisees must provide at least 50 per cent of the total investment in cash.

How do you get a bank loan for your franchisees? You may not have the financial capacity to guarantee a franchisee's loan. But if franchisors can afford to buy back inventory – and if they have 25 to 30 units and a track record – a convincing letter of comfort to the bank may do the trick. Such a letter would provide reassurance to the bank that the franchisor would monitor the franchisee's progress, and prioritize payment of the franchisee's debts to the bank over what is owed to the franchisor. The letter may ensure the bank that the franchisor will collect on the franchisee's inventory in case the franchisee goes into default.

## GOVERNMENT FINANCIAL ASSISTANCE

### A. Background and Benefits

Various levels of government pump billions of dollars each year into financial assistance for all stages and needs of business development. In the past, many such programs focused on the manufacturing sector and overlooked the retail and service businesses typical of franchising. But these days, job creation and training are high on the government's political priority list. And today more jobs are being generated in the service sector than in any other. While the focus may soon change, it is certainly worth taking the time and energy to explore this potential source of funding.

In the past, grants and packages that some viewed as bailouts were popular. Today, government programs have moved away from leading in financial assistance and toward supporting and assisting promising businesses. Typically, government funding supplements your equity but does not replace it. It shares the financial risk in situations where the risk would be too high for private funding.

Although you can sometimes get a term loan or equity financing from government programs, more often you will be able to arrange financing that complements your existing funding.

Typically, this financing will be in the form of medium-term debt that accepts higher risk and offers lower-than-market interest rates in return for a share in the success of your business. These lower rates can reduce a franchisor's risk, because they shelter you from exposure to increases in interest rates or a business downturn. Instead of a profit-based bonus, governments aim to see their return in the form of benefits to the economy.

Financial assistance from government can play a key role for franchisors in bridging a  financial gap or finding a more flexible repayment schedule than those available from other lenders. Compared to the private sector, the benefits of using government financial assistance include:

- fewer or possibly looser requirements for collateral security

- less equity required in the business

- less need to find financing from elsewhere

- potentially lower cost to loan

- more likely to be patient and supportive through bad times

- more likely to subordinate its position to other lenders

- their willingness to accept higher risk than other sources of financial assistance in exchange for a combination of financial and social returns

You may be eligible for government financial assistance if:

- you are financing a business or closing a financial gap
- you are restructuring for international competitiveness
- you require or currently employ workers who need training or retraining.

## B. Forms of Government Funding

Government funding is available in many different forms and hundreds of programs.

### (i) Small Business Loans

Under the federal Small Business Loans Act, banks administer government guaranteed loans of up to $250,000 to small businesses. These loans can be ideal for a new franchisee – and may form part of a bank franchise program – because the government guarantee on the majority of the loan reduces the bank's risk. Businesses with sales up to $5 million are eligible.

### (ii) Business Development Bank of Canada (BDC)

Formerly the Federal Business Development Bank, the BDC changed its name in 1995 to support and finance emerging business. As a federal agency, it most often acts as a supplementary lender to Canadian business. Because it lends when conventional lenders will not, the BDC typically charge one to two per cent higher interest for assuming higher risk. The BDC's services of interest to franchisors include:

- Working capital. It provides loans to small- and medium-sized businesses, to a maximum of $100,000.

- Patient capital. It provides loans to early-stage businesses that have a unique product or service and excellent growth potential. The maximum amount is $250,000, with a flexible repayment schedule. The charges include a royalty on sales plus a base interest rate.

- Venture loans. This is a type of financing for a growing or expanding company, or for a management buy-out or to develop export markets. Loans range from $100,000 to $1 million, and charges include a base interest rate plus a royalty on sales or a premium linked to business performance.

- Venture capital. Through its Venture Capital Division, the BDC provides equity financing to small- and medium-sized companies.

*(iii) Other forms of government funding*

Other government funding is offered through federal and provincial programs in the form of:

- Grants. These are often established to stimulate job creation, and there is no requirement to repay.

- Subsidies for wages. The government pays for all or part of a new employee's wages. Many such programs are offered through Employment and Immigration Canada.

- Subsidies for training and education. Some

programs cover management training for business owners.

- Subsidies for consulting services. You can get financial assistance for marketing, research or other areas of business through Statistics Canada, Industry Canada, or External Affairs and International Trade Canada.

- Tax and other concessions. These can include tax incentives for people to invest in your business. An immigrant investor program, for instance, will grant landed immigrant status to people from other countries who invest a certain amount of money in an approved investment.

- Government contracts. The government is a big purchaser of products or services. Supply and Services Canada has information on selling to the government.

## C. Where you can Find Sources of Government Funding

All levels of government have assistance programs, including federal, provincial, a few municipal governments, and some Crown Corporations.

### (i) Canadian Business Service Centres (CSBCs)

CSBCs are a joint venture between federal and provincial governments and are designed to provide one-stop-shopping for information on government programs. Each CSBC offers access to almost 900 federal and provincial programs. Check your phone book for addresses and phone numbers.

# Financial Information Systems

Financial information systems – including a franchisor's internal financial information system and procedures, the franchisees' systems and an accounting manual – should provide information on how well your franchise system is operating. These systems can help you monitor franchisee performance and take corrective action when danger signs arise.

When financial information systems are working well:

- franchisees are able to report accurate and timely data

- the franchisor can manipulate and analyze the data

- the franchisor can closely monitor each franchisee's financial health as well as the health of the overall franchise system

- the franchisor can keep watch for early warning signs of potential problems.

## A. Franchisor's Internal Financial Information System

Like any business, you need to set up your own financial systems and procedures – systems and procedures that must be compatible and standardized. As franchisees provide you with their financial data, your financial information system has to accommodate the input of the data, and then allow you to perform analyses and comparisons and to prepare reports. This data, especially sales volumes, form the basis of royalty calculations that you must verify to ensure accuracy and compliance with expected figures. If your business will comprise corporate and franchised outlets, be sure that your financial information system can handle data from both kinds of operations.

Your financial information system is a valuable resource to improve system performance through benchmarking. A practical historical guideline range or objective can be established as a goal for operating a store.

Every choice you make, such as the accounting time periods and the accounting software you use, will affect:

- franchisees' accountants and bookkeepers

- reporting requirements for franchisees

- franchisees' computerized point-of-sale and accounting systems

- the operations manual.

## B. Who does the Franchisees' Accounting?

Should you keep the franchisees' books? Franchisors who choose to do their franchisees' accounting say that the advantages include control, consistency and timeliness. They like to be able to walk across the hall and get the information on any store they want at any time. What's more, centralized accounting lessens franchisees' paperwork burden and lets them concentrate on running the business.

But centralized accounting may not even be an option for you. Early stage franchisors may find it difficult to do. And there has to be a lot of trust to persuade franchisees to give up control of their books.

In any case, whether you choose to centralize this function depends on a number of key factors:

- Do you have enough head office resources to take on the growing responsibility?

- Do you have the financial sophistication?

- Do your franchisees trust you enough?

- Can the franchisees meet your reporting needs? Do you need reports once a week, every two weeks or monthly?

- Are your franchisees capable of producing meaningful information on a timely basis?

## C. How to Handle the Books

There are a number of different ways that you can manage or assist franchisee accounting. The following suggestions are organized by franchisor involvement, from most to least. The franchise agreement should specify the option you choose, the fees for accounting services, and whether or not those fees are purely on a cost recovery basis.

- The franchisor can perform franchisee accounting on a fee for service basis. Your internal personnel then issue monthly statements to the franchisees. Economies of scale mean that your franchisees pay less for these accounting services than they would pay to an outside supplier.

- The franchisor can perform day-to-day franchisee accounting on a fee for service basis as above, but franchisees hire their own accountants for monthly and year-end statements.

- The franchisee can purchase accounting services from a franchisor-approved list of suppliers. A franchisor could, for instance, give franchisees a list of eight accountants with whom the franchisor has negotiated services on behalf of the franchisees. These accountants are familiar with your business requirements, and will each take a specified maximum number of franchisees.

- Your franchisees can be on their own. You would specify reporting requirements, formats and frequency.

## D. Reporting Requirements for Franchisees

In large organizations, a franchisor will electronically poll each franchisee's system nightly to capture key data such as sales. But this may not be economically feasible, and some franchisees may resent this level of control.

Nonetheless, you need reliable, timely and consistent information from your franchisees. Having each franchisee report data differently will be difficult, time consuming and costly. Franchisors can waste a lot of time having to reformat data and check accuracy. It is important for franchisees to use a common system to keep records and report data. And their accounting periods and data formats have to match.

The type of reporting you require should mirror your operational guidelines and reflect both the nature of your business and the key factors you want to monitor.

Timeliness is critical as well. You should be able to review reports weekly, or at least monthly. If franchisee reporting slips a period or two with no response from you, your franchisees may begin to see regular reporting as unnecessary. This can result in not detecting poor performance on the part of the franchisee, to the point where corrective actions are too late to be effective.

Good system administration procedures and monitoring to ensure compliance will avoid such problems. You should document your approach to meeting your reporting requirements in the franchise agreement, and clearly articulate the consequences of non-compliance.

Your financial information system is a critical tool for monitoring franchisees. It can provide you with a well-organized and timely monitoring and control methods to generate reports that will flag dangers before they turn into problems. And it will provide consistency in reporting, to make comparisons meaningful.

## E. The Accounting Manual

Your accounting manual sets out the procedures and requirements that franchisees must follow. If your systems are designed well and presented effectively in this document, franchisees will accept them. Your systems should clearly represent a low-cost, easy-to-use solution to their record keeping requirements.

Your accounting manual should include:

- all financial data you expect to be reported
- reporting format
- frequency of reporting
- acceptable accounting practices
- step-by-step procedures from data entry (in other words, the cash register) to final reports
- list of accountants.

The franchisees' chart of accounts may be smaller than yours, but it should be the same. This will make it easier for external accountants to review your books and for you to compare your system performance to others in your industry.

## F. Franchisees' Systems: Accounting and Point-of-Sale Systems

A uniform accounting system is ideal. Franchisees could do their own accounting using an accounting system provided by the franchisor. However, depending on the complexity of the business, franchisees may use their own accounting system to maintain their records.

Point-of-sale systems are fast becoming a necessity as well. They ensure that consumers' experiences are the same across the chain of stores or units. The customer should not experience a scanner system in one store and a mechanical cash register in another. In addition, one system-wide networked point-of-sale system enables the exchange of various data between the franchisor and the franchisee.

If you use either a point-of-sale system or an accounting system, make sure it will eventually be able to link electronically to the other. If you prescribe a point-of-sale system, for instance, it should be able to link electronically with a variety of popular accounting packages.

Using either of these systems have the advantages of:

- easier transmission of data: even if transmission is not electronic, statements can be faxed to head-office

- consistency of data

- system support: it is easier to support and update the system if all franchisees are on it.

## G. *Automating Financial Information Systems*

You may be in the early stages of franchise system development, with relatively unsophisticated financial information systems. But if your franchise system grows, you will eventually want to simplify procedures, ease paperwork and reduce costs by automating more of the financial reporting. Automating processes and implementing new systems and procedures need not be overly disruptive to your business if you ease the transition by:

- ensuring consistency of financial reporting across franchisees in both data and format
- establishing comprehensive requirements at the outset; adding reports and other features later steals time and energy and creates frustration.

## TROUBLESHOOTING STRATEGIES TO AVOID FAILURE

### A. *Financial downside of franchisee failure*

The costs of franchisee failure may include:

- terminating a lease, or paying rent until you find and set up a new franchisee
- taking over leases on equipment and fixtures
- buying back a franchisee's inventory which may be stale or overvalued
- loss of royalties
- legal fees

Add to these intangible goodwill costs of harm to your corporate image, plus the loss of financial and human resources that could have been better used to help other franchisees.

## B. Benchmark for Success

You can kick your franchise system's performance up a notch by benchmarking. This requires you to set up key measures, such as sales per square foot, sales per man-hour, or wages as percent of revenue, that can be shared internally but anonymously among franchisees. You can break these measures down by department or categories. You can also benchmark franchise system performance to other companies or industry standards. Standard charts of accounts can make such comparisons easy.

Typical financial measures used for monitoring include:

- sales and same store sales growth
- gross profit
- total expenses
- salaries and other expenses as a percentage of revenue
- net profit
- franchisee's equity
- sales as a percent of salaries
- sales per square foot
- accounts payable
- credit and collections
- inventory: levels, turns, value, and aging.

Different businesses will have specific "danger zones" for key measures. These "hot buttons" or "key indicators" are not a one size fits all proposition; they are specific to your industry.

So it is safe to use the standards and benchmarks for your particular industry, taking into account the anomalies specific to your franchise system. Many retail franchisors monitor franchisee equity to make sure it does not drop below 30%, for instance, because they want to ensure that the franchisee stays financially committed to the franchise and is not taking money out of the franchise to start another business.

### (i) Look for danger signs

Here are a few common danger signs and symptoms – and their possible causes.

- Late or delayed royalty payments. Since cash is your lifeline, you need to look at the situation of a franchisee who is short of cash very closely. Examine the top line (sales) as well as costs. Look for low sales, of course, but the problem might be caused by excessive personal expenditures by franchisees, overdrawn accounts, accounting errors, excessive debts, or even misappropriation of funds.

- Low net profits. This could be caused by high interest rates, low gross margins, low sales, high hidden costs, or poor expense control.

- Low gross margin. Look to low productivity, poor inventory control, shrinkage, bookkeeping errors or poor pricing.

- Low sales. Many factors could be afoot: not enough inventory, impeded access (road closure, mall renovation), need for store renovations, ineffective merchandising, uninspired salesmanship, key employee off sick, cost cutting on staffing or repairs or strong competition.

• Too much inventory. This may be due to poor sales, poor inventory control, or hoarding stale inventory.

• Not enough inventory. Poor inventory control, shrinkage or shortage of cash could be to blame.

## C. The Lender's View

The bank or other financial institution that holds franchisees' debt usually does not see franchisee trouble until a loan payment is missed. Banks prefer working together with the franchisees and franchisor to develop an acceptable turnaround plan. But the bank cannot discuss a franchisee's situation with the franchisor unless the franchisee has provided a letter of consent.

## D. What to do – Before the Business Fails

You have been monitoring your franchisees, and your systems and procedures have alerted you to danger signs. You have responded, but still a franchisee is in financial difficulty. What do you do?

This situation is different from dealing with an under-performing corporate store, where head office can bring in another manager or dictate new methods, because the franchisee is a separate legal entity.

Like many franchisors, you probably take seriously your responsibility to support franchisees. Here is how you can help:

- Check the franchise agreement. What does it permit you to do? What are events of default, remedies, franchisee obligations, franchisee cure periods?

- Consider how this particular franchisee responds to offers of help. Strong franchisor/franchisee relationships are key to dealing with troubled franchisees. If franchisees perceive their relationship with a franchisor as good, they are more likely to cooperate, regardless of the franchise agreement.

- Reassure the franchisee that you will try to help, and that you want work together to find a solution. If you have a good track record with turnaround situations, or if you have never closed a franchisee, say so.

- Establish and agree in advance on the payment priorities: they have to pay, in order, rent, bank loan, royalty. These must be paid before the franchisee takes home one dollar.

- Defer payments of royalties or advertising for a period of time.

- Convert missed payments into a loan on the condition that repayment will be through terming it out. The franchisee gets to stay if current payments are maintained.

- Be constructive. Do not say, 'You are doing poorly, you have not paid me so I am going to terminate your franchise agreement.' Instead, say, 'you have not paid me. I am sure you have a good reason for that. How can I help you build your business so you can pay me?'

- Work with the franchisee to construct a turnaround plan.

- Recognize when to cut your losses.

## E. Keeping the Franchisee Involved

Some franchisors prepare a step-by-step action plan for how they are going to correct problems, and then force it on their franchisees. This strategy does not work well as some franchisees resent it.

It is far more productive to build trust by instead saying, 'you are the owner of this franchise. What are you going to do about it?'

Get your franchisees to put their plans and solutions on paper. Like many businesspeople, franchisees may be great at fixing immediate problems but have difficulty with long term planning. By asking them to put pen to paper, you can force them to think through the problem for themselves.

## ACKNOWLEDGMENTS

This chapter could not have been written without the assistance of:

- **Claude Beaulieu** – Founder of Sports Experts, Member of the board of directors, *The Forzani Group Ltd.*

- **Robert Goodwin** – Business Leader, Home Services, *Service Master of Canada Limited*

- **Gerry Gordon** – Director of Franchising & Retail Development, *Yogenfruz Canada Inc.*

- **Anne MacPhee** – Director of Real Estate, Franchising & Construction, *Grand & Toy*

- **Wayne Parent** – President, *Nutrition House Canada Inc.*

- **Thomas G. Quinn** – Executive VP and COO, Franchise Retailing, *The Forzani Group Ltd.*

- **Garry Wood** – President, *Bell Distribution*

- **Daniel Farmer**, Sr. Manager, National Franchising Market, *Royal Bank of Canada*

- **Charlie Scrivener** – General Manager, National Franchising Services, *CIBC*

- **Craig Slavin** – President, *Franchise Architects*

- **Asghar Husain** – Manager, *Deloitte & Touche LLP*

- **Kerry Buller** – Researcher, *Deloitte & Touche LLP*

# CHAPTER 3

*By: Larry M. Weinberg*
*Cassels Brock & Blackwell LLP*

## THE LEGAL ASPECTS OF BECOMING A FRANCHISOR

### PURPOSE AND OUTLINE OF CHAPTER

This chapter will cover the basic legal issues which arise in franchising. It includes a discussion of the following:

A discussion of the basic legal structure which governs the relationship between franchisor and franchisee; and

The contractual framework, including a detailed discussion of what is in a franchise agreement and why.

The regulatory framework in Canada, and most notably, franchise legislation in the Provinces of Alberta and Ontario will be discussed in the next chapter.

## BASIC LEGAL STRUCTURE OF THE FRANCHISE RELATIONSHIP

Of the many methods available by which to distribute goods and/or services to the ultimate consumer, business format franchising is probably the most complex from a legal perspective. "Business format" franchising is the term used to describe the traditional franchising business model that most people are familiar with today. It essentially involves a license to market a product and/or service through use of a business method, including use of a business name, the methods of doing business (often called the "system"), the overall look of the business, and access to certain benefits (such as access to suppliers and group advertising). Certainly, when most people think of a typical franchise, they envisage this most common form, namely the "business format" franchise.

To begin with, there must be a "licensor" (called the franchisor) who grants to a licensee (namely, the franchisee) a "bundle" or package of the various rights described above to be used in conjunction with one another, for the purposes of delivering the products and/or services to the consumer. The franchisor may be the owner of these various rights, or it too may license them from another person, with a view to sublicensing the rights to franchisees.

Before proceeding further it will be helpful to provide some discussion on the legal aspects of the relationship between franchisor and franchisee.

### A. Contractual Relationship

First and foremost the franchise relationship is one based in contract, with the rights and obligations of the parties determined by their agreement. The franchisee's rights to use

---

*First and foremost the franchise relationship is one based in contract, with the rights and obligations of the parties determined by their agreement.*

---

of the bundle of rights described above are granted pursuant to a written contract, and thereby creates a legal relationship. And apart from some terms set by specific franchise laws, the relationship between the franchisor and the franchisee is truly one established and governed by the terms of the contract, the franchise agreement.

One Court has described the practical nature of the franchisee and franchisor relationship, as follows:

Franchise businesses provide a system that an independent entrepreneur would have to spend some time and money developing alone. Franchising is a method of distributing or marketing a service or product through a system. A franchisor grants a franchisee the right to carry on a business in a prescribed way.

Franchises offer advantages to the entrepreneur trying to start a business primarily the reduced risk of failure because a proven system of marketing is involved. It is often easier to finance because bankers often look more favourably on a proven concept than on an unproven one. In addition it offers training and support, purchasing power that the independent often lacks, advertising clout and reduced distress because many of the ins and outs of business operations are already developed. The disadvantages are loss of independence because of required adherence to a particular system and payment of royalty fees... over and above the franchise purchase cost.

While so-called "joint venture" franchises exist, it is most typical for the franchisee to be a non-related or arms length business entity. In fact, it is the hallmark of most franchises that this independence exists.

## B. *Fiduciary Relationship*

A fiduciary relationship is one where one party owes special duties to the other, the most common being the relationship between partners, and that between a trustee and beneficiary. The hallmark of such relationships is that the person in the position of power, the fiduciary, owes a special duty of care towards the weaker party. It is generally thought that the relationship between franchisor and franchisee is not a fiduciary relationship. When the Court is faced with the standard relationship with franchisors imposing strict terms and conditions to expressly protect their system, it is likely that these restrictions are not sufficient to impose a fiduciary relationship upon one of the parties. And while even the Supreme Court of Canada has affirmed this general view, courts have left open the possibility that, in the right factual situation, a court could find that a franchisor and franchisee have a fiduciary relationship.

## C. *Employment Relationship*

The essence of the franchise relationship is the notion that the franchisee is an independent contractor, a distinct legal entity, and is not in an employer-employee relationship with the franchisor. That being said, most franchise agreements and franchise systems seek to place numerous controls on the way in which the franchisee operates. This can range from things such as dictating everyday operating procedures, determining the level of inventory to be maintained, or even prescribing the amount of money that a franchisee can take out of the business by way of salary.

In some situations where franchisors have set too restrictive standards, the contract and the practical aspects of the relationship have led courts to decide that what has really been created is an employer/employee relationship. Accordingly, a well versed franchise lawyer will counsel a new franchisor not to try and control every single aspect of the relationship. Many of these cases arise where the "franchisee" claims employment type severance and other benefits for having been terminated.

## D. Statutory Relationship

As will be discussed in the following chapter, both the Provinces of Alberta and Ontario have legislation that specifically regulates the sale of franchises.

In addition though, these statutes affect the nature of the relationship between franchisor and franchisee by imposing on both parties a duty of "fair dealing" towards one another. Both statutes provide that this duty of fair dealing includes (but is not necessarily limited to) an obligation to act towards each other in "good faith" and in a "commercially reasonable manner".

These statutory duties affect all other aspects of the franchisor/franchisee relationship, although the extent to which such a duty will be used to override or merely supplement provisions of a contract are not yet known. It will only be known if and when a body of case law is built up providing judicial guidance on the scope and meaning of these statutory duties.

In addition, the Civil Code of the Province of Quebec has for some time imposed certain duties of "good faith" on parties to all contracts, including franchise agreements.

It should also be noted that in interpreting the statutory duty, at least one court recently noted that a duty of good faith already existed at "common law" and that the Ontario statute merely codified the existing law. This could therefore very well be the situation in all other provinces.

## THE PARTIES IN THE FRANCHISE RELATIONSHIP

Perhaps for the lack of any better analogy, the franchise relationship is often compared to a marriage; essentially a "partnership" in a true, but not necessarily legal sense. The parallels between a marriage and a franchise relationship exist because both the franchisor/franchisee and the married couple depend upon each other for their continued well being (financial and otherwise). As well, the relationship is intended as one that will continue for a long period of time, to the mutual satisfaction of all involved.

A further attribute of the franchisor and franchisee relationship, which makes the marriage analogy particularly relevant, is the sometimes unfortunate reality that misunderstandings tend to increase in number, duration, and intensity the further one gets from the "honeymoon". In fact, it is quite common to refer to the period of time just before and after the franchise is purchased, and begins operation, as the honeymoon period.

The growth of franchising over the last thirty or so years, as a means by which goods and services are distributed to the customer, can likely be attributed to the fact that when franchising works, it works quite well. In these situations, both the franchisor and the franchisee are relatively successful, in the sense that the arrangement meets their respective expectations.

Disputes and problems in franchising often arise when one or both of the parties have very little appreciation for what franchising is all about. It is often simply naiveté at work,

---

*The franchise relationship is often compared to a marriage; essentially a "partnership" in a true, but not necessarily legal sense.*

---

meaning that one or both of the franchisor and franchisee has not done their homework so as to fundamentally understand the relationship, and what one needs to have in place to make franchising successful.

A more detailed analysis of the parties, and some discussion of what motivates them and their expectations, follows.

## A. *The Franchisor*

From the franchisor's point of view, the benefits of franchising can often be seen in terms of the ability to "grow" a business or chain through the use of another's capital. Commonly, while the franchisor does not have access to the funds needed to build outlets, individual outlets can be paid for or financed by individual franchisees.

More directly though, the franchisor often benefits monetarily through the receipt of upfront license or franchise fees, being an initial payment for the use of the system know-how and trade-marks, an ongoing royalty (usually based upon a percentage of gross revenues) for the continued benefits of being part of the franchisor's system, as well as the benefits derived from the increased sale by the franchisor of inventory to franchisees.

The prospective franchisor embarks on franchising often with the belief that it is creating an immediate and guaranteed revenue stream. The potential monetary benefits will certainly appear attractive to the novice franchisor, especially when the market rate for initial franchise fees is typically between $20,000 to $50,000, in some instances, and some franchisors command a royalty equal to nine or ten percent of the franchisee's gross sales.

However, there is an entire body of knowledge that a prospective franchisor must acquire, usually quite quickly if they are to be successful, to ensure that the franchise system operates as it should. This franchise body of knowledge is distinct and separate from the other body of knowledge that one would hope the franchisor has command of even before embarking on franchising at all, namely expertise as to the underlying business.

For franchising to succeed, the underlying business must already be successful. It is the only foundation upon which a solid franchise system can be built. A poor business will not become successful simply by franchising it, and the entire system can suffer if the franchisor needs to devote time and energy to fixing its own business at the expense of time and care needed by the franchisees.

There is a way of doing franchising right, to put the right team of staff together, to thoroughly educate franchisees and to have expertise in choosing locations and negotiating leases. Typically the most successful franchise chain is one that can be completely systematized.

The franchisor needs to set proper criteria for choosing the most qualified candidates and to not grow too rapidly, without proper regard to geographic constraints (especially in a large, thinly populated country like Canada). A motto which all franchisors should adhere to is to that they be able to "service what they sell." Namely, the franchisor should strive to offer the necessary services to the franchisees who are already in the system, so that they will continue to believe in the franchisor's abilities, and pay royalties because they see value in what they are paying for.

Initial fees merely compensate the franchisor for time and expense in properly sourcing and training the franchisee, as well as the other costs incidental to setting up a franchise such as site selection and lease negotiation. The franchisor itself usually needs a significant amount of startup capital to start the process properly and to continue over the long term. Economic downturns tend to take their toll on franchisors who are themselves undercapitalized. When the next franchise cannot be sold, their source of funding disappears and soon, so does the entire franchise system.

## B. The Franchisee

From the franchisee's perspective, it is usually anticipated that the franchise will provide access to use of certain know-how which the franchisee could not duplicate on its own or in a manner which is economical. Many prospective franchisees are people who never previously operated their own businesses. They look to franchising as a happy medium, affording them the necessary degree of security, while offering the independence of an owner operated business.

For the prospective franchisee, the following are at least some of the specific benefits which are expected from any franchise system:

- information, training, and access to certain know-how in the operation of a business;

- bulk purchasing power for equipment, inventory and supplies;

- pooled advertising power;

- use of an established and recognizable name and trademark;

- system-wide innovation; and

- assistance in identifying and obtaining good locations.

Typically, in a developed franchise system, a prospective franchisee will be able to adequately investigate the benefits expected, and such an opportunity will often be viewed as one with less risk attached. A newer franchise system will, in contrast, be somewhat of an unknown commodity, less capable of being investigated through its prior actions, and it will therefore have a greater risk level attached. Of course, the purchaser may very well be willing to bear the greater risk when the opportunity exists to obtain a franchise in the early stages of its development, presumably at a lower cost.

This may appeal to many prospective franchisees, who are of course entrepeneurs by definition. That being said most successful franchisees cannot be "too entrepreneurial" such that they are incapable of taking direction and following a system.

Most established franchisors will present the franchise package of documents as non-negotiable and it is in fact a "take it or leave it" proposition for the franchisee. With respect to new franchise systems, the franchise agreement is in fact open for negotiation, and attempts are often made to minimize the risk inherent in an unproven concept.

## C. The "System"

Franchisors will typically refer to the "system" as an expression of all of the elements which, once put together in a package, the "business format", make up the franchised businesses operating under license from the franchisor. A typical definition of the "system" would include all of the various forms of intellectual property rights which the franchisor has combined to make their unique business. In many ways, the "system" is the third "person" in every franchise relationship.

Most franchise "systems" include most of the following types of rights, namely: trade-marks (the chain's principal business names), trade secrets (secret recipes and manuals), copyright (management programs and manuals) and trade dress (specially designed premises). Each type of property is, of course, somewhat different in nature, and each is subject to different protection by the law. Later in this book there is a chapter which discusses in greater detail franchising and the legal aspects of intellectual property.

## TYPICAL FRANCHISE DOCUMENTS AND COMPONENTS

Now, this chapter will continue by discussing those items which make up the basic components of the franchise agreement and related documentation.

It should be noted that, with respect to the Provinces of Alberta and Ontario, any discussion of the franchise relationship and agreement tells only part of the story. These two Provinces are the only jurisdictions in Canada which specifically regulate the sale of franchises. Generally, this legislation requires that a franchisor provide a "disclosure document" to a prospective franchisee before selling the franchise. Anyone dealing with franchising in these two Provinces must have regard to the applicable legislation. These laws also specifically govern the relationship between the franchisor and the franchisee. A more detailed discussion appears in the next chapter.

## A. *The Franchise Agreement*

As discussed previously in this chapter, the basic outline and structure of the relationship between franchisor and franchisee is established through the contract signed by the parties, namely the franchise agreement. Its purpose is to provide for each parties' rights and obligations, but necessarily leaving to the franchisor the ability to provide specific information about operation of the business to other documents, such as policies and an operations manual. In this section, we will examine the key components in the franchise agreement, and related documents.

### (i) *Parties*

For franchisors, simply deciding upon who is to be the franchisor can often be a complex question, involving corporate law and tax issues, in additon to issues stemming from any applicable franchise legislation. This can be made further complicated if the franchisor decides to control the leases for its locations, and use separate corporations for one or more of these leases. Clearly, franchisors need to consult with a number of relevant advisors before commencing to franchise, as any decision made will continue to have ever growing ramifications as more franchises are sold.

From a franchisee's point of view, some attention must be given to whether the franchise agreement is to be entered into personally or through a corporation. For tax reasons, it may be advisable to first enter into the agreement personally, take advantage of start up losses, and later roll the assets of the franchised business into a corporation. Typically, this will not be objectionable to a franchisor, as the franchisor will invariably require that a personal guarantee be provided of all of the obligations under all of the franchise related documents.

## (ii) Grant

Most franchise agreements are drafted on the basis that the franchisee is granted the right and license to carry on business, and use the franchisor's system and trade-marks, on a non-exclusive basis. The license may in fact be restricted to a particular site, location or territory.

## (iii) Term and Renewal

The franchise agreement usually specifies an initial term, which is often tied to the length of the lease for the premises in which the franchised business is to be carried on. However, and notwithstanding this most common approach, the length of the initial term should be related to the franchisee's initial investment and the time it will take to recoup this investment with some form of return. From the franchisor's point of view, a term which is too long can mean that they may be "stuck" with a poor operator.

The renewal of the franchise will invariably be subject to specific conditions, including the ability to maintain the existing or suitable alternate premises. The franchisor may specify other renewal criteria which could include the franchisee's obligation to:

- extend the existing franchise agreement, or execute the then current form of franchise agreement (which may or may not contain different financial terms);

- pay a renewal fee; and
- be in good standing under the franchise agreement.

Obviously, if the franchisor retains the ability to change the fundamental business terms of the franchise arrangement, the franchisee must be aware that this possibility exists at the outset of the franchise relationship.

## (iv) Exclusive Territory

Depending on the nature of the underlying business, it may or may not be appropriate to provide franchisees with exclusive territories in which the franchisor will not operate and/or license others to operate. As stated, however, a franchise is sometimes granted for use at a specific site only, with no restrictions on the franchisor's ability to carry on business or grant to others licensed use of the system. Even if an exclusive territory is granted, the franchisor will need to consider whether certain exceptions are warranted, such as the sale of products through other channels of distribution, including by way of the internet.

For marketing purposes, a newer franchise system will often grant large territories, which may in fact be inappropriate in the circumstances and a hindrance to future growth. At other times, territories are granted with little or no regard to the actual territory being given up. For instance, reliance on a radius clause of a certain number of kilometres may or may not be correct in any one circumstance.

Even if an exclusive territory is not granted, the franchisor who does not give due regard to the actual trading area of a franchisee, and allows the placement of other franchises in too close a proximity, is running the risk of future problems.

Lastly, maintenance of an exclusive territory can be made subject to various performance criteria. This type of arrangement is often the subject matter of negotiation between the franchisor and franchisee.

## (v) Location and Development of Site

Quite often, a franchise is sold without a location having been committed to. If such is the case, both franchisor and franchisee are well advised to insert a mechanism whereby the franchise agreement can be unwound if a mutually satisfactory site is not found within a set period of time

Once a site is located and agreed upon, the franchise agreement must deal with the development of the premises, whose responsibility this is to be, and the cost. Two approaches are typically employed. The first is where the franchisor provides the specifications and plans to a franchisee, who is expected to then be responsible for his or her own construction. The second, and perhaps more common approach, is for the franchisor to provide a "turn key" outlet, where in essence the franchisor becomes a general contractor and builds at the franchisee's expense. Most franchise agreements will be quite "open ended" about the franchisee's payment obligations (i.e. by not providing a cap on overruns). Most franchisors will disclose as much detail as possible about construction cost issues, in order to later avoid problems. For franchisors operating in the Provinces of Alberta and Ontario full disclosure of expected costs is required.

From a franchisor's point of view, the attractiveness of constructing premises on behalf of franchisees is that it can ensure a consistent look to each franchised unit. As well, a franchisor should be able to build at a price better than would otherwise be available to a franchisee on its own, while still ensuring a profit.

In certain instances, and perhaps for reasons of financing, key pieces of equipment may be leased by the franchisee, either from the franchisor, or third party suppliers or manufacturers.

## (vi) Leasing of Premises

Various options are available in a franchise system where the leasing of a location is critical to the success of the franchised outlet. Historically, the generally held view was that, for reasons of control, the franchisor was best advised to lease the premises itself, and in turn sublease them to the franchisee. This would require the preparation of a standard form sublease as part of the franchise document package.

If pursuing this route, the franchisor's next decision is what to charge as rent. Most franchisors simply flow through all of the costs under the head lease, while a minority will increase the amount payable and secure this for themselves.

However, it is not simply enough to have a sublease. The sublease must be proper for the franchise situation. Worthy of note are provisions which ensure that any and all payments due to the franchisor under the sublease and under the franchise agreement (i.e. royalties) are deemed to be rent. This will allow the franchisor the right to exercise the remedies available generally to a landlord upon non-payment of rent. As well, the franchise documents should contain so called "cross default" provisions which provide, in both the franchise agreement and sublease, that a default under one agreement is a default under the other.

The obvious drawback of a franchisor leasing the location directly is the contingent liability attached to holding leases, and for this reason the "preferred option" has become less prevalent in the last decade or so.

An alternative method is for the franchisor to use another company, which it owns, to be the tenant of the franchised businesses premises, so as to shield the franchisor company from liability to landlords. Unfortunately, a lease holding company can itself present a problem in situations where one or more problem leases are held by a company whose other assets are desirable leases.

Another alternative method is to allow the franchisee to directly lease the premises from the landlord. Under this arrangement, the franchisor is not the franchisee's landlord. Consequently, the franchisor is not able to control the franchisee, or the premises, to the same extent. However in recent times, more and more franchisors are attracted to this type of arrangement.

A so called "middle ground" is for the franchisor to extract from the franchisee and landlord an agreement specifying that the franchisor has the option to assume the lease in the event of termination of the franchise agreement or lease. While this may give to the franchisor the contractual right to obtain possession, it is much less powerful than the direct rights of being a landlord. If a dispute were to arise, this third option would likely not be of as practical a benefit as being a landlord outright. The lease assumption option will require that a particular clause be inserted in the franchise agreement, as well as in the lease for the premises.

## (vii) Training and Assistance

While franchise agreements will not often provide much detail in terms of the franchisor's explicit obligations, it is typical to provide for a training program, during which the franchisor is obligated to train the franchisee, and perhaps its principals, in the elements of the franchise "system". The actual content of the training program will vary greatly between franchise systems, regardless of the strict contractual language.

The agreement usually provides that the franchisee must successfully complete the training program prior to being allowed possession of the franchised outlet. A mechanism is often inserted whereby the transaction can be unwound, and a franchisee will be provided some form of refund of monies paid, if the franchisee cannot successfully complete the training program.

A franchise agreement will sometimes deal with the "grand opening", and specifically provide that the franchisor will have staff on site to assist in opening the outlet. Agreements will also sometimes require that the franchisee expend a certain specific amount on an opening local advertising campaign.

Ongoing training and assistance by the franchisor are usually specified to be in an amount as determined by the franchisor as being necessary in the circumstances. This ongoing training and assistance can take the form of site visits, classroom time or franchisee meetings and conventions. While a certain amount of ongoing assistance and training can be expected to be paid for out of royalties, extraordinary training or assistance is often charged back to franchisees, who would also be responsible for travel and related expenses for such training.

## (viii) *Franchisee's Ongoing Obligations*

A franchise agreement should provide for an extensive list of the franchisee's ongoing obligations as a licensee of the system know-how and trademarks.

The agreement would typically specify strict operating procedures, and the setting and maintaining of standards through various operating manuals and policies provided over the course of the term to the franchisee. One can well appreciate the franchisor's need for such strictness, in order to ensure uniformity throughout the franchise system, for the benefit of the franchisor and all franchisees. Provisions can be included which will allow the franchisor to modify the system and require the franchisee to institute these changes when indicated.

An often important aspect of the franchisee's ongoing obligations is with regard to the purchase of inventory and supplies. It is not uncommon for a franchise agreement to specify that the franchisee is obligated to purchase all inventory and supplies from the franchisor or its designated suppliers, who effectively then control the price and all payment terms. Often enough the entire franchise concept is built on the sale of unique products or services, in which event such requirements are well understood. However it is not uncommon for complaints to arise when a franchisee questions the profits made by the franchisor on the sale of inventory and supplies to its franchisees, especially if franchisees can obtain the same or similar products at cheaper prices elsewhere.

In certain instances it is appropriate for the agreement to specify that the franchisee is allowed to purchase some or all of its inventory and supplies elsewhere, subject to approval by the franchisor regarding the quality of the alternative sources.

If the franchisor intends to retain the benefit of volume purchases, rebates and discounts for its own benefit, then it is well advised to explicitly provide for this in the franchise agreement. In the Provinces of Alberta and Ontario such disclosure is mandatory. Otherwise, a franchisee will often expect that these benefits are to be passed on to the franchisees.

Beyond the items discussed above, a franchisee's continuing obligations could also include:

- A requirement that a particular individual devote his or her full time and attention to the operation of the franchised business;

- Maintaining the continued condition and appearance of the franchised outlet;

- Hours of operation;

- Use of standardized packaging, advertising and other materials;

- Maintenance of specified insurance;

- Implementation of warranty and promotional programs; and

- Maintenance of any necessary permits, licenses or other approvals.

As stated, the method of operation will often be imparted to franchisees through an operating manual, typically defined as being made up of any and all written and electronic materials provided to the franchisee. The manual may, therefore, go on to provide for other standards in the operation of the franchised outlet, and will invariably be subject to confidentiality restrictions.

## (ix) Fees and Royalties

As indicated at the outset, a franchisor will typically charge to franchisees an upfront initial fee, payable on execution of the franchise agreement or over a short period of time, in exchange for the rights and licenses granted under the franchise agreement. While franchisors may view this amount as a source of profit, knowledgeable franchisors understand that the initial franchise fee compensates the franchisor for the time and money expended in sourcing franchisees and ensuring that they open for business. Most front end fees will range from twenty to fifty thousand dollars, with fees higher than that being considered out of the ordinary.

In contrast, and regardless of whether expressed or implied, most understand that the payment of royalties is in exchange for the ongoing use of the trademarks and system, as well as the ongoing services and assistance provided by the franchisor. These royalties can be calculated by any number of means, including a flat amount paid at a specific time, an amount based on a increasing or sliding scale, but most typically it is calculated as a percentage of a franchisee's gross revenues.

While many franchisors are quite scientific in the amount of royalty to be charged, others base them simply on what the market will allow. The royalty rate can range anywhere from three to ten percent, with service related businesses tending to extract a higher amount.

The franchise agreement will of course need to specify the time and method by which royalties and other amounts are payable. Royalties are typically paid on a weekly or monthly basis, the more frequently the better for the purposes of maintaining control over the franchisee's operation of its business. More and more franchisors are also trying to institute electronic fund payment systems, and if desired, this should be specified in the agreement.

## *(x) Reporting and Audits*

As can be expected, a franchise agreement should contain very strict reporting, inspection and audit rights and obligations. If the franchisor's revenue is based on a percentage of the franchisee's sales, the franchisee will be obligated to report its sales and financial position on a frequent basis.

A franchise agreement will also provide for such requirements as: the franchisee's obligation to maintain complete and accurate books and records, a certain type of cash register or computer system as dictated by the franchisor, allowing for credit and other ongoing reference checks, and invariably, requiring delivery to the franchisor of all completed tax returns.

## *(xi) Advertising and Packaging Materials*

Franchise agreements will usually contain very specific provisions regarding the scope and content of advertising and the franchisee's obligation to contribute a specified amount to an advertising fund or pool in common with other franchisees. Apart from making contributions to an advertising fund, some thought needs to be given to whether a franchisee should have to spend certain further amounts on local advertising.

Most standard form franchise agreements contain provisions regarding the advertising obligations of both the franchisor and the franchisee. Regardless of who is to initiate any advertising of the franchised business, or the system generally, it is clear that it is the franchisor's system and its component parts, the franchisor's trade-marks and other proprietary rights, which are being advertised to the public. As such, a franchise agreement will typically contain a provision regarding ownership of the contents of the advertising materials.

Similarly, the franchisor's trade-marks may be displayed to customers in packaging or other materials, which will reflect upon the franchisor's property. As such, the franchise agreement will often contain a provision with the intention of governing usage of these materials.

## (xii) Non-Disclosure and Confidentiality

A typical franchise agreement should contain a specific provision obligating the franchisee to maintain all aspects of the system in confidence. As well, and in order to protect against harm caused to the system by employees of the franchisee, it is sometimes recommended that franchisees be obligated to have any key or critical employee execute a confidentiality and non-disclosure covenant in favour of the franchisor.

## (xiii) Restrictive Covenants

Franchise agreements invariably attempt to protect the integrity of the system by containing two forms of restrictive covenants, one which prohibits the franchisee from competing against the franchised business, directly or indirectly, during the term of the franchise agreement, and secondly, a covenant which restricts such activity following expiration or termination of the franchise agreement for a specific period of time and in relation to a specific geographic territory. Both "in term" and "post term" non-competition covenants attempt to safeguard the system and its proprietary components from being copied or being used in competition with the franchise system. So long as they are properly drafted and executed, these restrictions should also be enforceable against the principals of a franchisee corporation.

It is to be noted that a post termination restrictive covenant is sometimes difficult to enforce. The courts begin with the historic legal proposition that any covenant in restraint of trade is void as against public policy, while only thereafter recognizing that reasonable restrictions are allowable. What is "reasonable" is dependent upon the facts of any one given situation.

## (xiv) *Intellectual Property and Restrictive Covenants*

Over and above the issue of trade-marks, the elements that make up most franchise systems are essentially a body of know-how or other intellectual property rights belonging to the franchisor. The intellectual property aspects of the franchise agreement are easily the subject matter of a more lengthy treatment. For this reason this topic is covered in a separate chapter appearing later in this book.

## (xv) Transfer

It should not be unexpected that at some point, a franchisee may wish to sell its existing franchised business. In turn, the franchisor should be concerned about the identity of any transferee, keeping in mind all the effort that was put into sourcing the original franchisee.

For these reasons, the franchise agreement will invariably permit a transfer, but be very strict in specifying the criteria which need to be met before a franchisee will be allowed to assign the franchise agreement. Most importantly the transferee will need to meet the franchisor's standards for the granting of franchises, and be approved of in advance. It is not unheard of for a franchise agreement to specify that it is not assignable, or if assignable, then the franchisor can arbitrarily withhold its consent. However, this can obviously affect the marketability of franchises at the initial stage, and a franchisor is better advised to have strict but reasonable conditions for sale. The franchisor's level of actual involvement in the transfer process can also trigger certain disclosure obligations pursuant to applicable franchise law.

Because of the time and expense to be incurred by a franchisor on a transfer, a reasonably considerable transfer fee is not uncommon. It may even approach the amount of the initial franchise fee or a percentage of the franchisee's gross selling price. Upon approval, the franchisee or transferee will be obligated to pay for the franchisor's direct expenses.

The transferee may also be required to execute the then current form of franchise agreement. The agreement should specify whether the "then current form of franchise agreement" can have substantially different financial or other terms than the original. However, if a new form of agreement is to be signed, issues can arise under the franchise disclosure laws of both Alberta and Ontario.

The franchise agreement will usually be freely assignable by the franchisor.

## (xvi) Defaults and Rights on Termination

A franchise agreement will usually not provide for any express rights of termination on the part of the franchisee. Such provisions will typically only be found in a carefully negotiated franchise agreement where a new system is involved.

In contrast, a carefully drafted franchise agreement will go to great lengths to specify the events of default on the part of a franchisee. These can range from the typical insolvency related breaches, to non-payment of monies owing, and other failures to abide by the system. Except in the most extreme of cases, it is always suggested that a reasonable cure and notice period be provided.

On termination, it is very common for the franchisor to be provided with a right to purchase any and all of the franchisee's business related assets, at a price determined by reference to a formula.

### (xvii) Post Termination Provisions

Upon termination, the franchise agreement and the franchisee's right to operate the franchised business come to an end.  While it is not the intention of this chapter to discuss all such post termination provisions, it is important to note that these are often designed to ensure the franchisee ceases the use of any and all elements of the franchise system.

### (xviii) Security

A franchisor who is also an on-going supplier of inventory and supplies is well advised to take a security interest in the assets and undertaking of the franchisee's business.  On a practical basis, the franchisor's interests will be subordinated to the security interest granted to the franchisee's bank or similar start up lender.

Even where the franchisor is not an on-going supplier, it is becoming more common for franchisors to insist upon the grant of a security interest in order to secure the payment of any and all amounts owing.  The franchisor must weigh the rights gained as a secured creditor with the costs and administration time in maintaining registered security interests against an ever growing number of franchisees.  If for no other reason though, being a secured creditor can have its advantages with the right to appoint a receiver and manager over the franchised business on a default.

### (xix) Guarantees

Regardless of the franchisee's form of ownership, personal guarantees will invariably be required, and where the franchisee is acquiring a single unit franchise, this is not typically the subject of any negotiation.

Pursuant to specific legislation which exists only in Alberta, any guarantee taken will require independent legal advice, and execution of a prescribed form of certificate by the guarantor and counsel. The failure to abide by this law can affect the enforceability of the guarantee.

### (xx) "Boilerplate"

Similar to most comprehensive and complicated contractual documents, the franchise agreement will have lengthy "boiler plate" provisions dealing with various issues of interest usually only to lawyers at the time the contract is being enforced. However, the presence or absence of any once of these types of provisions can certainly affect one or the other party's success in pursuing and achieving a legal remedy.

## B. Other Documents

In the previous discussion on the elements of a franchise agreement, reference has necessarily been made to various collateral documents which may form part of the franchise package.

By way of summary, these can include:

- A lease or sublease of premises;
- Equipment leases;
- Software licenses;
- A lease assumption agreement;
- A general security agreement;

- Agreements relating to the construction of the franchised business premises;

- An agreement relating to secrecy and confidentiality; and

- An operations manual

In addition, and as will be discussed in the following chapter, the Provinces of Ontario and Alberta require that no franchise may be sold unless and until a disclosure document has been provided by the franchisor to the franchisee, and a prescribed waiting period has elapsed.

## C. Pre-Sale Materials

A franchisor will typically disseminate a package of sales information to numerous parties who express interest in the franchise system. In all provinces the franchisor will then often require that a confidential personal history application form and net worth statement be provided to the franchisor detailing the personal history and financial background of the prospective applicant.

It is at this stage that in all provinces, except Ontario, the franchisor will attempt to identify those truly interested by requiring the execution of an application agreement, and in certain circumstances the payment of a good faith deposit, in order to release further information about the system and the pro-forma franchise documents.

A typical application form should deal with the following matters:

- the amount of the good faith deposit;

- when and on what terms it is to be refundable;

- whether it is to be fully or partially refundable;

- basic confidentiality provisions;

- a reasonable time period within which the applicant has to consider, accept and/or reject the franchise opportunity; and

- authority to conduct credit checks.

Application agreements and the pre-contractual taking of deposits are no longer permitted in the Province of Ontario, and are restricted in Alberta. In Ontario, no money may be paid or agreement signed relating to the franchise until at least 14 days have elapsed from the franchisor giving any franchise candidate a disclosure document. In Alberta the deposit that may be taken is limited to a nominal amount, and the application agreement may address only certain issues, namely a fully refundable deposit, confidentiality and the designation of a location or territory.

As will be discussed in the next chapter, in both Ontario and Alberta, the most important pre-sale document is the disclosure document prepared and disseminated in accordance with the applicable franchise laws.

## D. Master Franchises and Development Agreements – Variations on a Theme

This chapter deals primarily with issues arising in single unit franchising, where a franchisee is typically an owner/operator of the franchised business. There are, however, variations to this approach, some of which are more complicated and sophisticated than others. Two of the more common are so called "master franchise arrangements" and "development agreements". There is often not even an agreement on what these two terms mean, but for the purposes of this chapter the following are some notable characteristics.

## (i) Master Franchising

Most often, the term master franchising refers to the franchisor granting to a "master franchisee" a larger territory within which to sub-franchise outlets to third parties.

Master franchising is often used as a means by which to enter a new market, or country. For this reason, it is quite well known in Canada as a means by which American retailers and businesses entered the market.

The benefits of master franchising are the ability to turn over many of the franchisor related functions to a party who is local. So, many master franchisees take over such functions as franchisee recruitment, site selection, construction and operational support, within their market. That being said, one of the drawbacks for the franchisor is the loss of control, and the requirement to share in royalties being paid.

## (ii) Development Agreements

A development agreement is essentially a contract whereby a franchisor grants to a franchisee the exclusive right to open multiple unit franchises within a defined territory, over a fixed period of time. Typically, the franchisee will be required to enter into a single unit franchise agreement with the franchisor, for each franchise opened.

Unlike master franchise agreements, development agreements do not generally allow for the franchisee to sub-franchise to other parties any of the unit franchises within the defined territory. However, some arrangements have characteristics of both master franchise and development agreements in that either the franchisee can open units on its own or sub-franchise.

Unlike single unit franchise agreements, the contents of which are discussed above, master franchise and development agreements are typically not signed in a standard form. They are, instead, often unique to the circumstances, and more heavily negotiated between the parties.

# THE MARKETING OF FRANCHISES

## A. General Considerations

The sale of a franchise is markedly different from the sale of other businesses. To most people the sale of a franchise is the sale of a license whereby another is provided with the opportunity to use a business format, various operating systems and a name. To others, most notably in those jurisdictions where franchising is regulated by legislation, the sale of a franchise also involves the sale of an investment opportunity. As stated earlier, and on a purely practical level, a franchise is viewed as a "marriage" whereby each of the participants brings their own unique qualities to the relationship, and where the success of one is dependent on the success of the other.

At every stage of the selling process, and because of the unique aspects of what is being sold, opportunities exist whereby both verbal and written materials are used to induce someone to purchase the franchise. As with the sale of any business or investment opportunity, the potential exists for misunderstandings, exaggerations and misrepresentations. In the correct circumstances those doing the selling can be, and often are, held accountable in law if those verbal or oral statements are characterized as inducements, and turn out to be either untrue or incorrect.

A franchisor has to understand that, notwithstanding the use of disclaimers, unsubstantiated or ill-founded claims can, and often will, come back to haunt the franchisor. This is certainly true in any jurisdiction (in Canada, Ontario and Alberta) where franchise legislation mandates disclosure of all material facts, and provides remedies for misrepresentations and the failure to fully disclose.

Of course, the areas where such representations can be made are perhaps too numerous to count. They can include the preparation and subsequent reliance on pro forma financial statements, statements regarding the financial health of the franchisor, the estimated costs of constructing a "turn key" operation, and the proven acceptability of the franchisor's concept in the marketplace.

Depending upon the facts of any one given situation, both franchisors and those acting on their behalf, can be held accountable. This is explicitly recognized in Ontario and Alberta's franchise legislation. Even where not expressly dealt with in a statute, the courts have at times even pierced the corporate veil and held the franchisor's principals jointly and severally liable along with their corporations because the franchisors had made numerous misrepresentations and acted in bad faith throughout the relationship. Clearly then, a franchisor ought to do all that can be done to avoid potential liability.

Firstly, of course, the information provided to prospective franchisees should be completely accurate. Secondly, wherever information is provided that is of a speculative nature, such as financial projections, the franchisor should ensure that they are properly prepared, based on reasonable information having regard to the particular franchise being sold. So, for instance, any assumptions made should be disclosed, and, as much as possible, the information should be gleaned from actual results of other comparable units. Both Ontario and Alberta now have quite detailed rules that must be followed in relation to the making of so called earnings projections. Thirdly, all those in the franchisor's organization must be thoroughly educated as to the potential pitfalls that await those who are overly zealous in the selling process. Fourthly, all prospective franchisees must be encouraged to seek out and obtain independent legal and accounting advice.

## B. Consultants And Brokers

In the sale of franchises, a franchisor may either attempt to maintain the selling process in-house, or use the services of consultants or brokers. Such brokers are typically quite experienced in the successful selling of franchises, and it is for this expertise that the franchisor will usually pay a handsome commission.

However, the new franchisor using the services of a broker is also placing a great amount of reliance on the broker to both screen potential candidates, and to advise the franchisor on each individual's suitability. Often the candidate's entire exposure to the franchisor or the franchise system will be through the broker, and the franchisor must ensure that the correct message is being given to the prospective franchisees.

If that seems of minimal importance, or if the franchisor believes that the use of the broker will shield it of liability, then it must be remembered that the broker is the agent of the franchisor, and pursuant to the law of agency, the franchisor (as principal) will be held responsible for the actions of the agent, notwithstanding that a specific statement may not be authorized, so long as the agent is apparently acting within the scope of their authority (namely, in the sale of franchises).

While it is always suggested that the broker's engagement contain a broad indemnity in favour of the franchisor, this may be of limited practical value when seeking to defend a lawsuit commenced by a disaffected franchisee.

Clearly, whether the selling process is maintained in house, or if brokers are retained, then the franchisor must do all it can to ensure that a factual and unexaggerated message is getting through.

## C. Basis Of Liability

It will not be attempted in this chapter to set out the full scope of the courts' views on the liability which may be found to exist from the sale of franchises. Suffice it to say, the Courts appear to be going to some lengths to find what they consider a "just" result.

In certain instances the courts may characterize the statement, whether oral or written, as a misrepresentation actionable on the theories of tort law. Depending on the type of misrepresentation, either "innocent", "negligent" or "fraudulent", certain legal consequences may flow.

In other instances, for example where a franchise agreement contains a complete disclaimer against the making of any representations outside the written words of the contract, the courts can characterize the statement as a "collateral warranty" or "collateral contract"; namely a contract wholly separate from the other. Thus, liability is found on contract principles.

Generally speaking, the seriousness of the misrepresentation or the collateral warranty will determine the nature of the legal remedies available to the injured party. If the misrepresentation is fraudulent or is of such a serious nature that it can be characterized as a "fundamental breach" of the contract, then the injured party will have the right to rescind the contract. Other, less serious breaches will give rise to an action in damages only.

The courts have expanded the potential for liability by finding it on the basis of "unconscionability". The franchisor might be restricted from relying upon a broad exclusionary clause if the franchisor's conduct is found to be unconscionable in law, such as where a franchisor knew the forecasts given were likely inaccurate and that the franchisee was relying on them. However, an exclusion clause may have an effect if there were guarded representations that were not untrue, not provided negligently and not intended by either party to be a collateral warranty.

Now, and as discussed in the next chapter, both the Provinces of Ontario and Alberta have legislation which can result in a far greater number of people than just the franchisor being liable for the accuracy of the information disseminated by the franchisor. In addition, these laws provide franchisees with a series of remedies including a right to rescind the franchise agreement and sue for damages, in the event the disclosure obligations were not correctly complied with, or in the event of a misrepresentation.

## A NOTE ON QUEBEC

Most of the foregoing discussion on the law and business of franchising is applicable throughout Canada. Because of its reliance on a Civil Code of law, and language differences, an exception relates to franchising in Quebec. So, while many franchised companies operate in exactly the same way throughout the country, and the fundamental concepts are the same, there are subtle legal differences that one needs to be aware of. For this reason, most franchisors entering the Quebec market should take advice from knowledgeable Quebec based counsel.

# CHAPTER 4

*By: Larry M. Weinberg*
*Cassels Brock & Blackwell LLP*

## AN OVERVIEW OF
## CANADIAN FRANCHISE LAWS

### INTRODUCTION

Canada's federal system places constitutional responsibility for private contractual matters in the hands of each of the country's ten provinces. Hence, any activity in relation to laws directly regulating the franchise agreement can come only from the provinces. In contrast, competition law and trade-mark law each falls under the purview of the federal legislative authority, and accordingly, consideration needs to be given to certain specific federal statutes.

Therefore, in Canada there would appear to be little if any concern that the federal government might attempt to regulate franchising in some way. In addition, to date, only two provinces have seen fit to pass legislation that is specifically directed at the regulation of franchising. These two, the Provinces of Ontario and Alberta, are also a study in contrasts. Alberta was the first to pass such legislation, in 1971, and based its original legislation on that passed in California. In 1995 Alberta moved away from a statute requiring registration by franchisors with a government agency, and introduced one that is essentially based upon providing mandatory disclosure.

On the other hand the Province of Ontario passed its first franchise specific legislation in the year 2000, with the most important disclosure related provisions coming fully into force on January 31, 2001. While an attempt was clearly made to provide uniformity and consistency in these two pieces of provincial franchise legislation, there are some important differences.

The situation in Canada is to be contrasted with the United States where franchise laws exist at the federal level, and in 16 states.

Apart perhaps from the advent of the Internet based e-commerce revolution, the passage of franchise legislation in Ontario is the most important recent development affecting the business and law of franchising in Canada. The purpose of this chapter is to provide the reader with an overview of these laws and developments.

---

*The passage of franchise legislation in Ontario is the most important recent development affecting the business and law of franchising in Canada*

---

## THE PROVINCE OF ONTARIO

The *Arthur Wishart Act* (Franchise Disclosure), 2000 (the "Ontario Act") is the name given by the Ontario government to the recently passed statute regulating the sale of franchises in that province. It is for the most part a "disclosure" based statute, with however some key "relationship" provisions, namely: a duty of fair dealing, the unrestricted right of franchisees to associate and organise, and the requirement that Ontario law govern in certain circumstances.

The *Ontario Act* incorporates a fairly expansive definition of "franchise" that should encompass most traditional franchise operations in Ontario. Notable is the absence of a concept that a franchise fee must be paid, instead specifying that a franchise is defined as a right to engage in a business where the franchisee is required, directly or indirectly, to make a payment, continuing payments or a commitment to make payment(s) to the franchisor. Such payment(s) must be made either as a condition of acquiring the franchise, in the course of operating the business, or as a prerequisite to commencing operations. Hence, even the ongoing obligation to purchase inventory at a bona fide wholesale price likely meets the payment threshold. Additionally, the *Ontario Act's* definition of "franchise" requires either that:

(a) the franchisor grant the franchisee the right to sell, offer or distribute goods or services substantially associated with the franchisor's trade-mark or other commercial symbol and the franchisor exercise significant control or gives significant assistance to the franchisee's operations; or

(b) the franchisor (or the franchisor's associate) grants the franchisee representational or distribution rights and the franchisor (or the franchisor's associate) provides "location" assistance.

Unlike other jurisdictions, Ontario specifically included in its legislation the obligation on both franchisee and franchisor to deal fairly with one another. Further, Ontario has sought to define the fair dealing standard by stating that it is defined as including a duty to act in "good faith" and "in accordance with reasonable commercial standards". This duty applies to both the performance and enforcement of franchise agreements. Notwithstanding these guidelines, it is difficult to say exactly what the duty of fair dealing encompasses. Reasonable commercial standards will vary with the commercial activity at issue. Although good faith is not a novel legal concept in Ontario, it can be characterised in many different ways. It remains to be seen how the courts interpret this obligation.

The *Ontario Act* protects the rights of franchisees to freely associate with each other and to join or form franchisee organisations without interference, restriction or penalty from franchisors.

The *Ontario Act* creates a statutory right of action for damages against specific persons who breach the duty of fair dealing, or where a franchisor interferes with a franchisee's right of association.

The disclosure requirements contained in the *Ontario Act* will likely have the greatest impact on both franchisors and franchisees. Franchisors will be required to provide prospective franchisees with a "disclosure document". The contents of this document must include the franchisor's financial statements and copies of agreements to be signed, and list in an accurate, clear and concise format, all "material facts", defined as follows:

*The disclosure requirements contained in the Ontario Act will likely have the greatest impact on both franchisors and franchisees.*

> "Material fact" includes any information about the business, operations, capital or control of the franchisor or franchisor's associate, or about the franchise system, that would reasonably be expected to have a significant effect on the value or price of the franchise to be granted or the decision to acquire the franchise;

The implementation of the disclosure obligations was delayed until January 31, 2001, so that the necessary Regulations could be introduced under the *Ontario Act*. These Regulations specifically deal with the content of disclosure documents listing certain mandatory information which must be included, such as: a detailed business background of the franchisor and its principals, information on previous criminal and civil liability, information about the franchisee's costs associated with the establishment and operation of the franchise, a description of financing arrangements that the franchisor offers to franchisees, a description of any restrictions regarding the purchase or sale of services or goods, a description of policies regarding franchise territories, information regarding any volume rebates and use of advertising funds, and information about closures of outlets. In addition, it must include a certificate, signed by the franchisor, or where franchisor is a corporation, by two officers or directors of the corporation, which states that the disclosure document contains no untrue statement of material fact, nor omits required material facts.

The *Ontario Act* also requires that any estimates of annual operating costs or earning claims must have a reasonable basis, and that the background information must be made available for inspection.

The *Ontario Act* stipulates that all information be "accurately, clearly and concisely set out" and creates deemed reliance by franchisees on information in the disclosure document and on any misrepresentation contained in it (subject to certain defences available to the franchisor).

The disclosure document itself must be delivered at least 14 days prior to the earlier of the parties' entry into any agreement relating to the franchise or payment of any consideration by the prospective franchisee. As a result, the parties cannot sign any agreement relating to the franchise during this 14-day "cooling-off" period, which would prohibit even a confidentiality agreement, and the taking of pre-contractual deposits by franchisors is no longer permitted.

Additionally, a franchisor must provide prospective franchisees with a "statement of material change", disclosing any "material changes" that occur prior to the earlier of the signing of the agreement or payment of any consideration by the franchisee.

The *Ontario Act* does contain exclusions, namely, a listing of certain relationships deemed not to be franchises. As well, it provides for a number of exemptions from the disclosure requirements for certain kinds of transactions. These include the renewal or extension of an existing franchise, the resale of a franchise by a franchisee, or where an additional franchise of the same kind is granted to an existing franchisee. The *Ontario Act* also provides for a "sophisticated purchaser exemption", applicable where a prospective franchisee is investing in the acquisition and operation of the franchise, over a one year period, an amount greater than $5,000,000. There is a further exemption available, upon application to the Ontario government, from the obligation to disclose financial statements as part of the disclosure document. To qualify, one must meet certain threshold levels qualifying the franchisor as experienced.

Franchisees are granted a statutory right of recission and a right of action for damages if the disclosure document or a statement of material change contains a misrepresentation or if the franchisor otherwise failed to comply with prescribed disclosure requirements. Potentially liable parties include the franchisor, but also the franchisor's associate, agent and broker, along with "every person who signed the disclosure document or statement of material change". Any of the potentially liable parties may be held jointly or severally liable, should they be found liable or accept liability.

It is noteworthy that the *Ontario Act* incorporates a fairly broad definition of "franchisor's associate". A franchisor's associate can include anyone who controls or is controlled by the franchisor, or anyone who is controlled by another person who also controls the franchisor. Additionally, a franchisor's associate must be either directly involved in the grant of the franchise by reviewing or approving it, or must exercise significant operational control over the franchisee.

The *Ontario Act* prohibits any attempt to contractually avoid the application of *Ontario Act*. Additionally, any purported waiver of the rights granted to the franchisee, or release of the obligations imposed on the franchisor, are invalidated by the *Ontario Act*.

## THE PROVINCE OF ALBERTA

Until the year 2000, Alberta was the only Canadian jurisdiction that had implemented legislation relating specifically to franchising. Prior to November 1, 1995, the province of

Alberta regulated the sale and offering for sale of franchises through its original franchise law, based on legislation passed in the state of California. In order to sell a franchise under that regime, one had to register with the Alberta Securities Commission Agency and file (and obtain approval for) one's "offering" document, namely a prospectus or so-called "statement of material facts." There were also ongoing requirements such as the renewal of the registration, which included the registration and renewal of salesman of franchises.

The current regime under the revised *Franchises Act*, (the "*Alberta Act*") took Alberta franchise legislation in a new direction. Under the present legislation, a franchisor is no longer required to register or file documents with a government agency in order to sell franchises.

In many ways the *Alberta Act* is similar to the *Ontario Act* which followed it both in time and design. For instance, Ontario followed Alberta's lead by including a franchisee's right to associate, and expanding upon Alberta's imposition of a fair dealing standard.

The definition of "franchise" is broad. To fall within the definition and therefore governed by the Act, it may be sufficient for the relationship to be defined in terms of a continuing financial obligation to the franchisor by the franchisee and significant operational controls by the franchisor, not just the mere payment of a franchise fee. As a result many distribution-type relationships could find themselves falling within the definition as a franchise. That being said, and unlike Ontario, the purchase of a reasonable amount of goods or services at a reasonable bona fide wholesale price is specifically excluded from the definition of a "franchise fee".

The most notable obligation in the *Alberta Act* is that franchisors are required to provide prospective investors with a disclosure document. This document must include copies of franchise agreements, financial statements and all material facts relating to the franchise purchase, including information on the franchisor, and those that fit within the definition of an "associate". Schedule 1 of the Alberta Franchises Regulation provides an outline of the minimum disclosure information required. However it is important for franchisors to include all of what would be considered material facts (as defined) to the prospective franchise transaction, regardless of whether it is identified in Schedule 1. Also, it is important to remember that each of the *Ontario Act's* and the *Alberta Act's* listing of minimum mandatory disclosure does not exactly correspond.

Under the *Alberta Act*, a franchisor is obligated to provide their disclosure document to the prospective franchisee at least 14 days before either the franchisee signs any agreement relating to the franchise, or the franchisee pays any money, whichever is earlier. Some exceptions may apply to both conditions. This includes the ability to prepare and have a prospective franchisee sign an agreement that requires a fully refundable nominal deposit and/or which requires confidentiality on the part of the franchisee. No such exception is available under the *Ontario Act*.

A franchisor is also required to provide disclosure pertaining to any subsequent material changes (as defined in the *Alberta Act*) to the prospective franchisee before he or she signs any agreement or makes any payment.

The liability for the contents of the disclosure, and particularly in relation to a misrepresentation or failure to disclose, rests on the franchisor and every person who signed the disclosure document, but unlike Ontario, the associate is not liable for the misrepresentation. To this end it is noteworthy that where the franchisor is a corporation, it must be signed by at least two directors or officers, or the lone director and officer, if there is only one.

The *Alberta Act* provides for a number of exemptions to the disclosure document requirements, including the renewal or extension of an existing franchise, the sale of a franchise by a franchisee, provided that the transaction is at arm's length from the franchisor, and the sale of a subsequent franchise to an already existing franchisee. This additional franchise must be substantially the same as the existing franchise to take advantage of this exclusion.

Lastly, a separate Exemption Regulation provides an exemption to disclosing financial statements, if the franchisor meets a test based on experience, size and number of franchises. In contrast to the procedure set up under the *Ontario Act*, a franchisor need only satisfy itself that it complies with the *Alberta Act's* exemption pre-conditions, and declare as such in the disclosure document.

## OTHER PROVINCES

At the time of writing there are no concrete plans by any of the other provinces to introduce franchise legislation. As might be expected, such legislation is not necessarily a priority on any legislative agenda, and each government and governing party, has their own priorities.

Of the ten Canadian provinces, nine operate under a common law system, which has its roots in the British legal tradition. The Province of Quebec, in contrast, has a legal system based on its own unique *Civil Code of Quebec* (the "*Civil Code*").

While the civil law features freedom to contract, the current *Civil Code*, which came in to force on January 1, 1994, broadened the intended protection of those perceived to be weaker contracting parties. This is noteworthy for franchising in that the *Civil Code* has implemented certain requirements relating to the notions of good faith in the performance of one's obligations and reasonableness in the exercise of one's rights.

One method adopted to protect weaker contracting parties is the characterization given to "adhesion contracts". Adhesion contracts are contracts in which the essential terms are imposed by a party, and are not negotiable. Most contacts one comes across in every day life likely fall into this category. In light of the definition, most franchise agreements, which are lengthy and standard-form in nature and whose essential terms are usually not open to discussion, may be characterized as adhesion contracts. Once a contract is found to be an adhesion contract under the *Civil Code*, the terms in such contracts which are: (i) incomprehensible or unreadable by a reasonable person; (ii) abusive; or (iii) considered to be "external clauses", will be subject to judicial review, and could be struck down. For instance, a franchisor's manuals are typically not disclosed until after execution of the franchise agreement, and yet are still often enforceable terms as against a franchisee pursuant to the franchise agreement. If found to be "external clauses", namely ones not available for inspection by the franchisee prior to signing the franchise agreement, their enforceability may be questioned.

## OTHER LAWS

It is beyond the scope of this chapter to detail all of the laws in Canada, and its provinces, which potentially could affect a franchisor and a franchisee. But, such a list would typically include laws relating to the leasing of premises, taking a security interest in the franchised business assets, trade-marks, competition law and laws relating to the protection of personal information.

# CHAPTER 5

*By: G. Lee Muirhead*
*Osler, Hoskin & Harcourt Llp*

## INTELLECTUAL PROPERTY IN FRANCHISING

### INTRODUCTION

The core of the franchise relationship is the grant by the franchisor to the franchisee of the right to market a product or service using the franchisor's trade-marks, trade dress, copyrights, know-how, and confidential business system. These types of rights are all referred to as intellectual property.

In a competitive marketplace with dozens of similar products and services, intellectual property may be the only thing elevating one product or service above its competitors, for example, a catchy trade-mark or slogan that the public remembers; a secret recipe that makes one pizza better than the rest; a superior computer software product that allows the franchisee to deliver the product or service more efficiently. The intellectual property associated with the franchise system

---

*In a competitive marketplace with dozens of similar
products and services, intellectual property
may be the only thing elevating one
product or service above its competitors*

---

is, therefore, among the most valuable of the assets of the franchisor. Unfortunately, since it is intangible, it cannot be protected from theft or damage like physical tangible assets. Some elements of intellectual property, such as trade-marks and trade dress, serve their purpose only if they are presented to consumers in wide distribution. Once in the public sphere, however, they can be easily copied and appropriated. Therefore, franchisors must maintain strict control over the use of their intellectual property so it does not lose its value. The following chapter describes different types of intellectual property which are relevant to franchisors.

## TRADE-MARKS

### A. Definition

The Trade-marks Act (the "Act") defines a trade-mark as "a mark used by a person for the purpose of distinguishing … wares or services manufactured, sold, … or performed by him from those … of others". A trade-mark may be a word mark such as KODAK, MCDONALDS, or COCA-COLA, or a design such as the "golden arch" design of McDonalds, or a phrase, such as WHERE DO YOU WANT TO GO TODAY?

## B. Protecting Trade-Marks

The purpose of advertising and promoting a mark is so the consumer will remember that mark when faced with a purchasing decision. The uniqueness of the franchisor's trade-marks is the primary means of distinguishing the franchise business from its competitors and identifying its products and services to the consuming public. A well known trade-mark tells consumers that when they see the trade-mark, they may safely assume they will be obtaining goods and services of a type and level of quality they have come to associate with the business. Unscrupulous competitors may take advantage of this by using the mark, or one which is confusingly similar, to sell their own goods and services. If consumers are deceived, the franchisor and its franchisees may suffer damage to goodwill if the competitor's goods and services are inferior, and even if they are not inferior, the franchise system will suffer damage in lost sales which are going to the competitor rather than the franchise system. Accordingly, to protect the goodwill of the franchise system, franchisors must protect their trade-marks.

### (i) Registered versus Unregistered Trade-marks

The owner of a registered trade-mark has the exclusive right across Canada to use, and/or license others to use the trade-mark for the products and/or services in association with which the mark is registered. This right is infringed when a third party uses the same or a confusingly similar mark. Owners of registered marks may restrain the unauthorized use of their trade-marks or confusing marks by bringing an action for infringement. To succeed, the owner must show that its mark is registered and that the defendant is using the registered mark or one which is confusingly similar. The owner need not go through the difficult step of proving public recognition of its mark, as this is assumed by virtue of the registration.

A party may acquire legally enforceable rights in an unregistered mark (so-called "common law" rights), simply by using it. However, the scope of common-law rights is limited compared to those flowing from registration. Also, enforcing common-law rights is more difficult and costly than enforcing registered trade-marks. To protect an unregistered trade-mark, the owner must bring a legal action based on the tort of passing off. This action is based on the principle that a third party should not unfairly compete with the trade-mark owner by passing itself off as the trade-mark owner, namely by using a confusing mark to misrepresent to the public that the third party's products or services are those of the trade-mark owner, or that there is a business relationship between the trade-mark owner and the third party.

In order to succeed in an action for passing-off, a franchisor must prove that:

(a) its trade-mark is recognized in the marketplace as identifying products or services of the franchise system (i.e. the public has come to associate the goods or services with the franchise);

(b) the defendant is using the same mark or one which is confusingly similar and, as a result, the public is likely to think that the defendant's products or services are those of the franchise system; and

(c) the franchise system has suffered or is about to suffer damage as a result of the defendant's activities.

Establishing proof of public recognition of a trade-mark is time-consuming and expensive. Additionally, a successful franchisor will only be able to restrain third party infringers in the geographic area where it uses its trade-mark and can prove such recognition. Therefore, to maximize their rights, and to reduce the costs of litigation, franchisors should register their marks with the Trade-marks Office and use and license the marks only in accordance with the Act. The existence of the registration will often serve as a very useful practical way of dissuading potential compeititors from misusing the mark.

## *(ii) Obtaining a Registration*

In Canada, an application to register a mark may be filed on the basis of actual use in Canada, proposed use, use and application of the mark abroad or registration of the mark in other countries. A mark that is applied for on the basis of proposed use will not be registered until the applicant has started to use the mark here. A mark that is applied for on the basis of a foreign application will not be registered until the mark is registered in the foreign jurisdiction.

The Act prohibits registration of certain types of marks. A mark may not be registered if it is: (a) primarily a surname; (b) clearly descriptive or deceptively misdescriptive; (c) the name of the products or services with which it is associated; or

(d) confusing with an already registered mark or an official mark. For example, SHINY PLATINUM would not be allowed as a mark for platinum jewellery as it is clearly descriptive. Nor could it be used in relation to silver jewellery as it would be deceptively misdescriptive of the wares. Surnames, while generally non-registrable, can be registered if the company has already established wide-spread and significant recognition in the name, such as MCDONALDS and can demonstrate this to the Trade-marks Office.

A trade-mark that includes a surname or descriptive words may be registered if the applicant disclaims the exclusive rights to the surname or descriptive part of the mark.

Trade-marks that are confusingly similar with a prior registration will be rejected by the Registrar and not registered. Confusion is determined by looking at a number of factors, including the distinctiveness of the marks in question, the nature of the products or services associated with the marks, the nature of the trade and the degree of resemblance between the marks.

Even where there is no prior registration of a confusing mark, the applicant may not be the party entitled to obtain the registration of its mark since the Act creates rules for determining who is entitled to register a mark based on first use or first application dates, in order to prevent registrations of confusing or identical marks by different entities. To attempt to ascertain whether there are prior registrations of or applications for confusing marks, it is advisable to have a trade-mark search conducted before filing an application for a trade-mark.

Generally, similar marks will be confusing if they are used for similar products or services. On the other hand where the marks are similar but the products or services are unrelated, they can generally co-exist without confusion. For example, the manufacturers of DOVE soap are unlikely to succeed in a complaint that an unrelated company produces DOVE chocolate bars because they are in two different markets. However, this is not an absolute rule, as a company with strong and famous marks may have such wide-spread recognition that a consumer would still associate it with that company even if in the new product was in a completely different field. The DOVE chocolate bar company would likely have been less successful had they attempted to market ESSO or FERRARI chocolates.

Once the application is filed, it is assigned to an examiner in the Trade-marks Office who conducts an independent search, reviews the application for compliance with the formalities requirements set out in the Act and otherwise for compliance with the registrability criteria discussed above. If the examiner thinks the mark is registrable, he or she clears it for advertisement in the Trade-marks Journal. Once the mark is advertised, third parties can oppose its registration. The most common ground of opposition is that the mark is too similar to a previously registered mark or one that was used but not registered before the applicant's rights to the mark arose. If there is no opposition, or an opposition is unsuccessful, the application is allowed and upon satisfaction of outstanding formal requirements, the mark is registered. The process of obtaining registration may take up to three or four years if difficulties, such as oppositions, are encountered in the process.

Once registered, the trade-mark registration is valid for fifteen years, and may be renewed for a further fifteen years, an indefinite number of times.

## (iii) Licensing and Use of Trade-Marks

It is possible for one entity to own a mark and for others to use it without affecting the owner's exclusive right to use a mark only as long as it continues to be distinctive of the products or services of the owner. In the franchise context, this means that the trade-marks must indicate to the public that the products and services sold in association with the trade-mark are those of the franchise system rather than those of an individual franchisee or a third party. This puts the onus on the trade-mark owner to be vigilant in making sure no franchisees use the mark in a manner to suggest they own it. Failure to protect a mark can lead to it becoming generic or non-distinctive, and the franchisor may lose the registration.

---

*The franchisor must have direct or indirect control over the character or quality of the products or services sold by the franchisee.*

---

Before June 1993, franchisors were required to register all franchisees as registered users of their trade-marks in order to maintain the validity of the licensed trade-marks. Now, the registered-user provisions of the Act have been replaced with a system of controlled licensing and the continued validity of the licensed trade-mark depends on the franchisor's control over the character or quality of the products or services sold by its franchisees in association with the licensed mark.

Licensing arrangements with franchisees should be in writing and incorporated into the franchise agreement. The franchisor must have direct or indirect control over the character or quality of the products or services sold by the franchisee. However, direct control is normally exercised by supplying proper use guidelines, approving samples of the products produced by the franchisee, visiting the franchisee's premises to inspect the franchisee's products or services, acting on consumer complaints and controlling the source of supplies to the franchisee. A franchisor may exercise indirect control by appointing an independent agent to exercise direct control over the franchisee.

Franchise agreements should also contain a mechanism allowing the franchisor to exercise such control on periodic basis (ideally by inspecting the franchisee's business operations) as well as the right to terminate for non-compliance. Franchisees must not be permitted to sub-license the mark without the franchisor's consent.

Franchisees should be required to maintain the distinctiveness of the trade-marks by using the trade-marks only in the form in which they were registered, and in the form prescribed by the franchisor. The franchise agreement should include a clear statement prohibiting the franchisee from altering or modifiying the mark in any way.

The Act also now contains a presumption of proper licensing if public notice is given that the trade-mark is being used by the franchisee/licensee under licence and the franchisor/trade-mark owner is identified. Therefore, franchisees should be required to post notices which identify the existence of the license. The fact that the franchised business is independently owned and operated is also important and should be disclosed at the premises so that the public will know the identity of the entity supplying the products and services in case of a liability claim. It is advisable to use notices on the product packaging, saying all trade-marks are owned by the franchisor and are being used under license.

Franchisors should be aware that under the Act, their franchisees have the right to demand that the franchisor/trade-mark owner pursue a third party for trade-mark infringement. If the franchisor/trade-mark owner refuses or does not initiate proceedings within 60 days, the franchisee may launch an action, naming the franchisor as defendant. This can be changed by contract, so franchisors should include in their franchise agreements that they have the sole right to prosecute third-party infringement of the mark.

In addition to having contract provisions, franchisors should develop trade-mark guidelines which give detailed instructions to franchisees on how to use and display the marks. The guidelines should address the following requirements:

(a) Use the marks in a distinctive format. A trade-mark that appears in lower case letters may appear to be a generic name for the type of products or services offered by the franchise system. A trade-mark should appear in a special typographical format, such as upper case letters or italics, in quotation marks, underlined, in bold face, larger font or different colour than the balance of the text in order to avoid giving the impression that it is a generic name. This is especially true when using word marks, for example in advertising copy; franchisees should be careful to always identify the word as a mark and distinguish it from the text;

(b) Use the mark as an adjective. The mark should always be followed by a word or phrase describing the particular product or service, e.g. "Able hamburgers". The trade-marks should not be used as an noun (i.e. "a full line of Ables"), as a verb (i.e. "Able your hunger"), or in the plural form (i.e. "Ables");

(c) Use a standard form of trade-mark notice. If the trade-mark has been registered, the franchisor should use the symbol ® following the trade-mark. If the trade-mark has not been registered, in Canada, whether or not the franchisor has applied to register

the trade-mark, the franchisor should still use
the symbol "TM" (or the French equivalent
"M/C" for "marque de commerce").

Franchisors must exercise their rights under their franchise
agreements and actually control the franchisees' use of the
licensed trade-marks.   The franchisor has the onus of
monitoring the use of the mark by franchisees to ensure
appropriate use.  Similarly, the franchisor must also be vigilant
in watching for unauthorized use of the mark by third parties.
Failure to protect the mark in either case can lead to it becoming
generic and non-distinctive, and at risk of expungement.

## TRADE DRESS

### A. Definition

To a large degree, the success of a franchise system depends
on the ability of purchasers to identify an individual franchisee
as part of the system.  Franchisors, therefore, attempt to adopt
unique appearances for their business premises, which may
include a variety of elements, such as a colour scheme of the
business premises, a building shape, the packaging of a product
or the style of uniform or dress of the sales force.   The
appearance, or "look", of a business or a product is commonly
known as trade dress.   Where trade dress becomes well
recognised and well accepted by the public, it may be at risk of
being copied by competitors.

### B. Protecting Trade Dress

Canadian courts have recognized that property rights exist
in unique trade dress and have, in certain instances, restrained
third parties from copying another party's trade dress.  As with
unregistered trade-marks, the way to protect trade dress is with
an action for passing off.  The franchisor must prove that the

trade dress is identified with the franchise system in the minds of the public. The first step, therefore, is to show that its trade dress is unique, is used uniformly in all of its franchised outlets, and that its franchisees are bound by the franchise agreement to implement and use the trade dress consistently. The franchisor must have the right in the franchise agreement to dictate the appearance of the franchised premises.

The franchisor must also prove the defendant has appropriated its trade dress. The court will consider the first impression created by the defendant's trade dress and will restrain its use if the court feels that the public will mistakenly believe that the business of the franchisor is in some way connected to the business of defendant. A third party will likely not be able to avoid liability for passing-off by simply changing some minor details of the franchisor's trade dress.

Finally, to succeed in passing off, the franchisor must prove that it has or will suffer damage. A franchisor who is able to prove a claim in passing-off may claim damages for any loss suffered as a result of the third party's activities. More importantly, successful franchisors also may obtain an injunction restraining the defendant from continuing to copy the franchisor's trade dress.

## COPYRIGHT

### A. Definition

In Canada, copyright subsists in every original literary, dramatic, musical or artistic work. In the franchise context, copyright may subsist in works such as advertising materials, operating manuals, computer software, graphics, and trade-marks consisting of a design or logo.

The owner of the copyright in a work has the exclusive right to produce or reproduce the work or any substantial part of such work, to perform the work in public, to transmit the work to the public by telecommunication, to publish an unpublished work and to authorize any such act. Pursuant to the federal Copyright Act, the copyright in a work is infringed when any third party, without the permission of the copyright owner, does anything that only the owner has the right to do.

## B. Ownership

The Copyright Act provides that generally the author of a work is the first owner of the copyright. An important exception to this general rule is that an employer is the first owner of copyright in material created by its employees in the course of their employment. This exception does not apply to works created by independent contractors. Therefore, a franchisor should require any contractors it engages to create any copyrights for it to transfer the copyright to the franchisor. The Act requires an assignment to be in writing and signed by the assignor.

## C. Protecting Copyright

Copyright subsists in original works independent of registration, which means third parties do not have a comprehensive database that they can search to identify copyrights. Copyright law, therefore, accepts the possibility that a protected work may be copied innocently. Accordingly, if an infringer of copyright has no actual knowledge that copyright subsists in a work, and no reasonable grounds for suspecting it does, the only remedy available to the copyright owner is an injunction restraining use by the infringer. This means the defendant would be forced to stop whatever activities were infringing the owner's rights, but the defendant would not be forced pay monetary damages to the plaintiff. However, if the defendant knew, or should reasonably have known, that copyright existed, the owner is then entitled to damages, an accounting of profits and delivery of infringing copies as well as an injunction.

Where copyright is registered, third parties are deemed to have had grounds for suspecting copyright subsists and the owner of the copyright is entitled to monetary awards. The process of registering copyright is simple and inexpensive and should be considered in order to ensure that the owner can claim financial damages for infringement. To obtain a registration, it is necessary to identify the author of the work, the title and nature of the work (for example, literary or artistic), whether and where the work has been published, and the owner of the copyright.

Franchisors who own copyright in materials used in the franchise system should also consider using a copyright notice on all published copies of such works. The appropriate notice includes the name of the copyright owner, the information that the work is subject to copyright and that unauthorized reproduction is prohibited.

## CONFIDENTIAL INFORMATION

### A. Definition

Confidential information consists of information which is owned by a person, is non-public and is of commercial importance to that person. Unlike trade-marks and copyright, confidential information is not protected by statute. The owner of confidential information must take whatever steps are available to him to protect the secrecy of the information since if it becomes public, it will be available for use by anyone.

Franchisors may have confidential information in the contents of their operating manuals and in other know-how of the franchise system.

## B. *Protection of Confidential Information*

Confidential information is protected in Canada at common law, and the Supreme Court of Canada in the case of Lac Minerals v. International Corona Resources Ltd. ([1989] 2 S.C.R. 574), held that confidential information is protected by reference to either or both of the law of confidential information and the law of fiduciaries.

In an action for misuse of confidential information, the issue is the nature of the information to be protected (not the relationship between the parties), and to succeed in such an action, a plaintiff must establish that: (i) the information to be protected is in fact confidential; (ii) it was communicated to a party in confidence; and (iii) it was misused by that party to the detriment of the plaintiff. Third parties may be liable to the owner of confidential information if they use confidential information disclosed to them by a party in breach of a non-disclosure obligation.

In an action for breach of fiduciary duty, the issue is the nature of the relationship between the parties. A fiduciary relationship was described in Lac Minerals as one in which the principal's interest depends on how the fiduciary uses a discretion that has been delegated to him. There are classes of relationships (such as directors and officers of companies) in which courts will impose a fiduciary obligation on one party to act or to refrain from acting in a specific way. Additionally, fiduciary obligations may arise out of the specific factual circumstances of a particular relationship. Fiduciary obligations include avoidance of conflict of interest and a duty not to profit at the principal's expense, and only the fiduciary (and not third parties who benefit from such a breach) can be liable for a breach of such obligations.

A franchisor who wishes to rely on the law of confidence in Canada, therefore, must demonstrate to the court that its information is confidential, how it maintained such confidentiality and the circumstances in which the information was communicated. Accordingly, a franchise agreement should outline the franchisee's obligations relating to use and disclosure of such information. It should require that confidential information be disclosed only on a need-to-know basis, and that the principals of a corporate franchisee, employees, and other entities who may receive confidential information from the franchisee, enter into non-disclosure agreements.

In addition, franchisors must continuously monitor use and protection of confidential information by all such parties, bearing in mind that a court will refuse to enforce agreements which attempt to impose non-disclosure obligations with respect to information that either never was confidential or has lost its confidential nature. For example, a franchisor that wishes to protect its secret recipes must ensure that they are kept secret by franchisees and their employees. Merely describing the recipes as confidential will not be sufficient to protect them. Similarly, information that is ascertained by reverse engineering a product will not be capable of protection under the law of confidential information.

Franchisors may also rely on the law of fiduciaries to restrain misuse of information where the franchisor can establish that the defendant was a fiduciary of the franchisor. Although absent special circumstances this action will not be available against franchisees, it may be available with respect to agents, employees, officers and directors of a franchisor.

## C. Termination of Franchise Agreement

Every franchise agreement must have clear provisions requiring the return and/or termination of use of all intellectual property. This clause should cover the return of all copies of confidential information, such as recipe books, company manuals and training materials and materials which are protected by copyright. Similarly, the franchisee should be obligated to stop using any trade-marks, trade dress or other intellectual property of the franchise system. If the franchisee is allowed to continue using the intellectual property, this may be seen as the franchisor waiving its rights to require the franchisee to stop and will impair the franchisor's ability to get pre-trial relief.

## SUMMARY

As franchising evolves as a way of doing business, the issues surrounding franchising become more complicated. Intellectual property rights are fundamental to the success of a franchise system and, given the nature of the franchise relationship, the protection and exploitation of intellectual property is more complicated than in more traditional business structures. Franchisors carry the onus of monitoring all franchisee uses of intellectual property associated with the business, and a well-drafted contract is a good starting point. Being aware of the legal issues relating to intellectual property also allows franchisors to communicate to franchisees the importance and necessity of this strict control. By developing procedures for the effective control of such rights, the franchisor will generate a great benefit for both the franchisor and all franchisees in the system.

# CHAPTER 6

*By: John Woodburn*
*C.J. Woodburn & Associates*

## MARKETING YOUR FRANCHISES - A PRIMER

### MARKETING – EMPLOYEES OR CONSULTANTS

Your concept has been created by you, through your efforts. At the start you and your business are one and the same. You've been involved in all aspects - operations, site selection and lease negotiation, construction supervision, operations, financing, hiring, merchandising, products, suppliers, etc.

Now you're faced with the dilemma/question - "Can I continue to grow the business on my own?" While it sometimes is possible to continue on your own for the first few locations - you'll probably soon find you're stretched in so many directions that things start to slip.

Now's the time to analyze yourself. What area or areas of the business do you do best and enjoy the most? Keep in mind that it's your business today and in the long run - but maybe it's time to hire or recruit help. In the infancy of a franchise system, some of your employees may be capable of playing a bigger role while still maintaining their own regular jobs. If so - great - as you know their strengths and can give them a chance to grow. Usually such employees are found in operations and can be involved in helping you in training and opening a franchise.

However, there may be skills that are required and that you don't presently have in your company. Two of the most common early need areas are marketing your franchise and real estate site selection. If you plan and are able to develop this expertise within your organization, this will typically be done through employees who devote their full time and attention to these franchise functions. They are usually employed on a salary and commission basis. If you don't have such expertise in house, find the best outside consultants available and hire them to assist you.

To get knowledge and experience, you'll want people with contacts in the industry, experience and a successful track record. To bring such expertise in-house by hiring fulltime employees is often too expensive for new franchisors. The usual alternative is to retain independent consultants, who work for a restricted number of clients. While this may involve some fixed costs, such specialists are usually paid the bulk of their compensation as franchises are sold.

When investigating who to retain, a franchisor should look for people who have had success and are recommended by their clients (who aren't competitors). Meet and evaluate them to determine the costs involved to ensure you are comfortable with them. It's important that you respect one another's roles and work successfully together. It will be the first time you are involving others as major contributors to the business's success.

It is not an easy step to take, but very necessary, so that you can concentrate on your strengths. You will want to establish an easy and open relationship with good reporting guidelines. You will need to be comfortable with their abilities.

Assuming the relationship works as it should, these consultants can bring years of success to your franchise system. Typically, as franchise systems grow, you may be able to afford employees with many of the required skills. Often outside consultants will be paid a monthly retainer, providing payment for ongoing marketing work, and a larger commission will be paid when franchises are sold. These contractors and you will have a fair two-way contract. Don't begrudge their rewards (payday) as they'll bring you a growing royalty stream.

Let's now review some of the functions involved in the granting of a franchise.

## MARKETING

Here are the steps and stairs in signing a franchise prospect.

(a) Find prospects.

(b) Educate/inform them.

(c) Qualify them. (Provide disclosure document if required)

(d) Present them to you for your evaluation.

(e) Work with the prospect's advisors (legal and accounting).

(f) Set up reference and credit checks and possibly, professional personality evaluation.

(g) Sign franchise agreements and associated documents (sub-lease or lease, confidentiality and personal property security agreements, etc.).

It may sound straightforward, but it requires experience and expertise to be successful.

Let's review some of the major hurdles involved in the start-up of a franchise system.

## COSTS AND CHALLENGES

You should be prepared for the costs involved to launch your franchise program such as:

### A. *Legal*

A knowledgeable franchise lawyer should draw up or review your franchise agreement. This is an absolute must! This agreement outlines your franchisee's responsibilities and also yours as franchisor. It will provide you with the tools to run, expand and if necessary, correct your system. Yet it should allow your franchisee to achieve his goals and be rewarded. Your sales force must understand and be able to answer prospective franchisees' and their lawyers' questions. For more details refer to the legal chapters of this book. Also, with the enactment of franchise legislation in Alberta and Ontario, you'll want advice on compliance with these disclosure laws.

### B. *Advertising*

Your sales team should assist in the creation of a "package" talking about your system. This will involve a written and pictorial presentation about your business that realistically showcases your sizzle! Those with expertise in their preparation will know from experience what sells, and what doesn't.

The creation and production of this package will include time and expense for writing, photography and production. Create a budget. Don't overspend to start with but make sure it's a quality story. It's the first taste of your business a prospect will have for he or she may have never seen you before.

## C. Finding Your Prospects

Today, anyone looking for a franchise business has a large number of options. They will have to decide what type of business they want and then further decide which ones may be best for them. Your advertising package, your sales team and your existing locations are the things that will have a prospect include your concept on their final selection list.

It's certainly helpful if you have an idea or profile of the ideal candidate for your business. This can be helpful in selecting the specific advertising vehicles you'll use.

Some methods for locating interested prospects are:

(i) Print media advertising – this can be national, regional or local (your target markets will narrow down the selection). Print media channels to be considered should include newspapers and trade publications.

(ii) Trade shows – these should provide a large number of interested prospects in a short time frame. Your show display will be a vital part of success in this approach.

(iii) Electronic – web sites and internet listings are increasingly productive today.

(iv) Non traditional – look for special ways to reach out based on your prospect profile.

> Don't overlook your sales team's networking opportunities.
>
> (v) Visibility – your existing locations can be a real showcase to develop prospects. Provide the means on site to turn customers into prospects.

Your sales team should have the experience to guide you in "creating your pitch". Advertising is expensive! Avoid image advertising and instead opt for messages that will catch a prospect's attention and tease them with the potential in owning one of your franchises (without, of course, misrepresenting anything).

## D. Early Franchisees

It's an accepted fact that your first ten franchisees will be the most important decisions you will ever make. These franchisees must operate profitably and successfully for you to grow past this number.

## E. Avoid Temptation

Resist the quick route of giving or selling franchises to friends, neighbours or relatives. These people may be easier to sell to, but they will be more difficult for you to work with because of your personal relationship with them. Also be careful of making special deals with early franchisees. They may come back to haunt you, and you could be obligated to disclose and discuss these arrangements with later franchisees.

One advantage of a good outside consultant is they can be the unemotional qualifier of applicants. Their recommendations should be based solely on the prospect's ability to enter and work in your system successfully.

Having said all these things, you can expect your early applicants to ask for special considerations in their agreements. They and their advisors will see you as an early franchisor. They'll look to receive special inducements or even cost breaks because, in their minds, there are a lot of early risks. Don't give away the future but be prepared for such requests.

### F. Qualifying Prospects

The final acceptance of a franchise applicant will be yours to make. When your sales force presents them to you for your review, it should have already been determined that they can financially and practically undertake the franchise.

### G. Disclosure

Once personal information has been received, and an applicant has been pre-qualified, you should be prepared to supply details about yourself, your company and your franchise. This can be embodied in a formal Disclosure Document as suggested by the Canadian Franchise Association or as required by law in the Provinces of Alberta and Ontario. You should note that in Ontario, for instance, you are not now permitted to collect any money (such as a deposit) nor have any agreement signed relating to the franchise until at least 14 days have elapsed from handing out a disclosure document.

Once serious applicants have shown their interest by supplying information about themselves, and received information about you, you can proceed to meet with them.

### H. Professional Screening

Keep in mind that the candidate having money to invest is, by itself, only one of the requirements that need to be satisfied in granting a franchise. In addition, your prospects need to show that they have the right commitment to be a franchisee.

There are now some very professional tests you can employ to understand your prospects. Consider using these tools from the start as they provide a scientific insight, in addition to your experience, gut feeling and personal meetings. For instance, they will help you assess whether a prospect is too entrepreneurial to be in business as a franchisee, as franchisees need to be able to follow a system directed by the franchisor.

## CLOSING

During the franchisee's due diligence period (often 14 to 30 days from the delivery of a disclosure document or a deposit) the prospect should be encouraged to:

*A. Talk With Franchisees*

Encourage them to contact existing franchisees to determine their satisfaction. You should provide them with a list of all your franchisees.

*B. Document Review*

Read thoroughly a blank copy of any sample franchise documents you'll require them to sign. These may include some or all of:

(i)   Franchise agreement

(ii)  Lease or sub-lease agreement

(iii) franchise disclosure document (where required)

(iv) Personal guarantee forms, security and confidentiality documents.

## C. Advisors

Provide a copy of all documents and proformas for review by their professional advisors (lawyer and accountant). Your consultants should be able to answer their standard questions and ask you for clarification on any special points they request.

## D. Financial Information

In Canada, unlike the United States, a franchise prospect quite often expects to receive an estimated cost budget and a conservative realistic sales proforma in advance of signing the Franchise Agreement. In Ontario and Alberta, providing an estimate of the costs of establishment and operation of the franchise in a disclosure document is now obligatory, and providing an earnings projection must be done in compliance with certain rules. They all have possible legal pitfalls. Regardless of whether it is mandatory or optional, the onus is on you to prepare this information carefully, and based on your actual experience. If you rely on assumptions, they must be pointed out and be reasonable. While the franchise operator is a major factor in success, truthful information is key. Invariably the franchisee's legal and accounting advisors will need to review this information on behalf of their client.

Experience dictates that a typical budget for a franchise would usually be provided to the prospect early in the process either in a disclosure document (where required) or in some other preliminary information. You and your sales team should have defined what must be invested personally by the new franchisee and how the balance can be funded. Most of your prospect's banking experience will be only with their past personal needs. Your sales team should be prepared to assist the prospect in preparing a business plan for their franchise, and once approved by you, take it to a banker experienced in franchising.

# FINANCING

Once the above steps have been followed, your prospect will be fully informed about your system and his/her legal, financial and operational responsibilities. Their decision and yours to proceed will allow you to sell/award them a franchise.

Most people who buy a franchise cannot afford to pay the full start-up costs from their own cash reserves.

Their accountant will advise them from where to draw their personal portion of the start-up costs (e.g. real estate, stocks, savings, family, etc.)

Your sales force should be ready and able to help the prospect develop a business plan. It should be complete and include cash flow projections for the first two years. This will become the operating guidepost for the franchisee once in business.

Many of the Canadian chartered banks have actively developed a franchise finance department at their head offices. These banks have sent their people "to school" to learn about franchising and to find out how to assess the support and comfort you'd give your franchisee. In your early days as a franchisor, the Canadian banks who are active in franchise lending will look at each application on its own merits and may want some comfort or back-up from you.

To leave an approved candidate to arrange their own bank financing often leads to frustration, rejection and delays. Most franchise prospects will only know and have dealt with a local personal loans officer, who may or may not have commercial and/or franchise banking experience. It's not unusual for such an approach to be unsuccessful.

## SMALL BUSINESS LOANS

In Canada the federal government has supported small business development by providing loan guarantees on certain small business loans.

While there has been some shifting of the terms over the last number of years, the general requirements are as follows:

(a) The applicants must be credit worthy for a loan on their own record and assets;

(b) The franchisee's own investment in the new business must be significant. The percentage of the total franchise cost which the franchisee must invest will differ among the banks from time to time. In general, both the banks and the franchisor want to make sure there is a strong personal financial commitment by the franchisee;

(c) There will be regular and trained management for the business;

(d) The franchisor has done the homework to ensure all parts of the franchise opportunity are properly analyzed and accounted for. e.g. location, lease, construction, etc.; and

(e) The franchisor will provide strong training and on-going support.

---

*To leave an approved candidate to arrange their own bank support leads to frustration, unsuccessful financial support applications.*

---

Once these are in place and details presented in a bank loan application with a complete business plan, a small business loan may be obtained as follows:

(i) The maximum loan amount is $250,000.00, which can be used to finance up to 75% of the cost of leasehold improvement, equipment and fixtures (The small business loan cannot finance franchise fees, or other "soft" costs);

(ii) There is a 2% one-time government underwriting / registration fee; and

(iii) An annual interest bonus premium of $1\frac{1}{4}\%$ is charged over the bank's loan rate. It is remitted to the government.

There are personal and business advantages – and some disadvantages - to taking this type of loan. These should be carefully explained to the franchisee. One distinct advantage is that the principals of a franchisee borrower will be required to guarantee only 25% of the original principal amount of the loan.

Once you've seen it's practical for a prospect to buy your franchise, you can proceed to execute your franchise documents, although often this is still conditional on financing and/or site selection.

---

*In food franchising it's universally accepted that the location is one of the most critical keys to a franchisee's success. In service industries, especially where the marketing philosophy is to go to the customer, location is not as important.*

---

# REAL ESTATE

## A. *Variance of Factors*

The location from which your franchisee operates will be dictated by many demographic factors such as:

- population
- street traffic
- income levels
- consumer profile of population
- square footage requirements; and
- facilities needed

In some franchises mall sites will be preferable, while in others strip or power centres can be successful. Some service industries can be either home based or located in industrialized areas or even in office buildings.

## B. *Style of Location*

The importance of the location will vary depending on the business. Some franchise systems are quite particular about the size and type of real estate needed for their locations.

In food franchising it's universally accepted that the location is one of the most critical keys to a franchisee's success. In service industries, especially where the marketing philosophy is to go to the customer, location is not as important.

Once you have defined the type of location you're after, the real estate hunt begins. Your style of location will define for you the recruitment of real estate consultants and the contacts they'll need to help you. If you are in the food business and want free-standing buildings, end caps or strip locations, the type of landlord/developer contact is different than if you want locations in regional or community enclosed shopping malls.

## C. Real Estate Commissions

Your costs for these services will also vary. Developers and landlords for non-mall locations will usually expect to pay an agent's fee. On the other hand, mall operators will not pay a real estate fee and your agent's fee must be included as a separate cost in opening your franchise. You may wish to include the real estate fee in your costs to ensure your agent has no commission preferences.

## D. Negotiations

The availability of reasonably priced space is cyclical depending on the current economic climate.

You decide what your rent cost parameters are in relation to your franchise, concept and sales expectations. For example, does increased retail traffic translate into higher sales? If so higher rent costs may still deliver good profit percentages.

In any event, always ensure you have final approval of a site, not your franchise prospect.

## E. Head Lease vs. Sublease

If location is an important ingredient to the success of your franchise, you may want to consider taking the lease yourself and subleasing it to your franchisee. This is referred to as "head manning" the lease.

It ensures you will always control the site and can drive a harder bargain on rent costs than could your new franchisee alone.

However, head manning also means you have a potential lease liability should your franchisee not fulfill the lease obligations. In Canada a landlord will usually look for the comfort of the franchisor's guarantee with or without that of the franchisee. The landlord may want to ensure in the early days that the comfort of the franchisor's head manning the lease will be through a company with substance. As you grow you may want to discuss with your advisors setting up a "real estate" company to hold the leases.

The actual details of obtaining market competitive lease costs and terms will require significant experience in the industry.

## F. Lease Term

The length of the lease is especially important in allowing your franchisee to recoup the investment made for leasehold expenses. It is for this reason that you usually find and want a ten year term or a five year term, with a five year renewal, in a retail environment.

## G. Use Clause

A professional landlord will be as concerned as you are to avoid overlapping use clauses between tenants' products, especially in multiple tenant areas. Therefore, it is suggested you develop a use clause that protects your major products and enables you to obtain the landlord's agreement not to allow other tenants to erode your core product sales.

### H. Co-Branding/Non-Traditional Sites/Alternate Channels

You may have already heard these franchise buzz words. Here's how they work.

#### (i) Co-Branding

This, in general terms, involves housing or locating two or more different franchises at the same location. Usually they will be complimentary and will not overlap during busy times of day and/or in products. An example is the combination of one franchise featuring coffee, and the second, pizza. Typically, the coffee franchise is busiest early in the day while the pizza franchise is busy at dinner time and the evening. With such a combination, greater revenue can be obtained from the same real estate.

In addition, it offers newer systems the opportunity to join its franchise with a more mature system, obtain better locations than it could on its own and access to established franchisees. Before you launch onto this road, make sure you study how the operations and selling functions mix. They are often complicated and need to be considered before embarking on such a venture.

#### (ii) Non-Traditional Sites

Many franchisors have, as mentioned, an established format with a required size and type of location. However, as the availability of traditional sites diminishes, because of factors such as market saturation, you may need to consider alternatives. For instance a franchise that has its traditional stores in free-standing buildings with a drive-thru and sit-down service, may also consider an alternative, such as a food service kiosk in a high traffic or mall location. Or, they may locate satellite locations in self-service gas stations. These are often serviced and staffed by a traditional location franchisee nearby.

### (iii) Alternate Channels

Another increasingly popular approach is for frachisors to start distributing their brand of products or services through channels of distribution other than their franchised outlets. One example is selling over the internet.

This can be complicated enough in a purely corporate store environment. However, it becomes even more complicated when distribution through alternate channels results in a franchisor, or others operating under the franchisor's authority, competing against the franchisor's own franchisees.

## PROFIT – A GOOD OR BAD WORD?

You've probably heard stories of financial conflicts between franchisors and their franchisees.

The first way to avoid this conflict is to make sure you have profitable franchisees. If your franchisee is being rewarded by a fair return for their efforts, you should have few realistic complaints.

Keep in mind that you'll be successful only if your franchisees are successful.

The second way to avoid conflict is to always be up front and provide adequate disclosure. If your revenue stream as a franchisor is exclusively through royalties - say so. If you also will get revenue (profits) from product supply or construction build out - say so.

Product rebates are quite typical in many franchise industry segments, like food, so do not try to hide it. (In Ontario now, such information must be disclosed.) Your new and existing franchisees will be primarily concerned that they can buy competitively from approved product sources. Make sure you choose your suppliers for quality, cooperation, service and regional strengths.

If you make a profit in building out the store - say so. The costs can then be a part of a prospect's evaluation and decision making.

Hard feelings and confrontations usually occur because the income of the franchisor is seen by the franchisee as making them uncompetitive or has been hidden from them. Reasonable franchisees will want you to be profitable, survive and lead but not by causing them hardships.

Similarly, if your franchise has another way of receiving its reward rather than a royalty percentage based on sales, declare it. In some product franchises such as bath and skin care, the franchisees are usually bound to buy products only from the franchisor. These products are bought at a net cost which includes the franchisors reward (margin). In both cases (the franchisor and franchisee) will want to ensure that costs are relative to quality in the market place, to ensure competitive product sales and profit.

## ADVERTISING FEES

Most franchise agreements require a franchisee to expend/contribute a percentage of their sales to advertising. Whether local, regional or national, these funds should be spent to increase awareness and store traffic.

What and how these programs work will vary based on your business, location and customer profile.

It is strongly recommended that advertising funds from franchisees be made payable to a separate bank account. Wherever possible invite franchisee representatives to have a voice in the direction of the advertising dollars. Also, require that your corporate stores contribute equally.

Make sure that you report annually to your franchisees on funds received and expended. If you direct some of your funds or even suppliers' rebates to this fund - show it. This openness will ensure your whole system works towards expanding your two-way relationship and hence sales.

In the early days of your franchise system you may need to invest in advertising yourself because of your small number of franchisees. Make sure your advertising efforts are directed to build franchisee traffic – not brand image.

## EXPANSION STRATEGIES

### A. Geography

One of your important decisions is where you want to expand. Is it to be close to where your office is? Will it be local, regional, national or international?

As a rule of thumb, plan to expand in areas you can easily get to and service. Too far beyond your reach will mean you have orphan stores because you don't see them as often as you should. Usually this results in underachieving stores and stores that vary or stray from your system.

It's sensible to stick close to home at first. As you grow your success becomes known. What is often then difficult is the ability to resist the siren song from afar.

(i)   Strong candidates from distant parts of the country; and

(ii)  Interested parties from outside the country.

The first recommendation is ensure you are strong and profitable in your home market. Expansion at a distance will draw you and valuable resources away from your home market. Franchising too far afield can be costly, in both time and money. It's especially troubling if it affects your home base.

## B. Area or Master Franchisees

As you spread across Canada you'll attract interest for what is called master or area franchises. Before being seriously considered, these individuals should have the following traits:

(i)   experience in business;

(ii)  good financial strength;

(iii) performance commitment – will open a quantity of locations in a defined timeframe - 1, 3 or even 5 years; and

(iv)  prepared to support their own locations in the territory they are provided.

You'll find more details in the legal section relating to this approach. In actual fact you are downloading your growth and reputation to your area or master associates. This may be good or bad.

From a marketing terminology, we consider the differences between these two expansion systems to be:

(i)  Area franchisees can open as many corporate locations in an area as they wish but don't have the rights to sub-franchise.

(ii) Master franchisees can open either corporate or sub-franchise locations in their geographic area.

Make sure you spell out how you'll share royalties, franchise fees and responsibilities between the two of you and their performance or location expansion responsibilities.

## SUMMARY

The marketing of your concept will be a major key to your expansion success. If you prepare yourself fully, select a sales team with confidence, be realistic in growth plans, you'll have a good start.

While expansion is important to you, always remember that when a prospect decides to join your team, it is probably the biggest financial and risk decision they have ever made. Respect this and ensure you deliver your knowledge and support to ensure their success.

# CHAPTER 7

*By: Kent Harding, Founder and C.E.O.*
*Kwik Kopy Printing*

## ONE FRANCHISOR'S JOURNEY

### OPENING COMMENTS

Franchising a business requires you to develop entirely new skills, and to look at your own business in a new light.

You find yourself pulled between keeping your store operating effectively and answering the numerous questions posed by your franchised store operators. Some of these questions are meaningful and require your dedication. The rest are meaningful to the franchisee and you must not shrug them off. There is no such thing as a dumb question.

Typically, in the beginning you have three to five locations. They might be run by friends, relatives or interested associates who think this is a good idea and who believe in you. However, they are also probably beginning to think that you don't know very much about their operation. They believe they are special, and their operation is different than your original store. There are several things they have found that work better than your method. You now must think in terms of building a non-adversarial relationship with your franchisee. You want to promote co-operation, a system for everyone's' benefit – customer, franchisee and franchisor.

It's time now for one very serious decision in your career: "What business are you in anyway?"

In my case, I had to decide whether or not I was in the printing business or in the franchising business. These two businesses are totally different. They require totally different disciplines.

I realized I was now in the teaching business. It was my job to teach people how to be in the printing business. It was pretty difficult being the best printer I could be – providing my customers with high quality printing and excellent customer service at a reasonable price – while also trying to keep my three initial franchises going in the right direction.

I was pulled in two ways: should I concentrate on getting that rush print order out the door for a very valued customer, or should I help my franchisee with his identical problem? Who was my customer anyway – was it the franchisee or the actual print buying customer?

---

*It was pretty difficult being the best printer I could be – providing my customers with high quality printing and excellent customer service at a reasonable price – while also trying to keep my three initial franchises going in the right direction.*

---

I asked myself, why did I go into the franchise business? I wanted to expand my printing company but could not invest further. Printing was a highly capitalized business and in order to have sufficient funds I needed to have additional investors. Franchising was a solution, allowing rapid expansion and the ability to reach more customers in a short period of time.

It was obvious to me that the only way I could rapidly expand my customer base was to have others contacting my customers. I could hire more salespeople, which required increased capital as well as training time. Or I could find people to operate my stores who had a definite drive, ambition and the motivation to do the best possible job of getting and keeping these new customers.

A franchisee is a person with his savings on the line and is committed to success. A businessperson who wants the comfort of a proven system supporting him as he worked toward shared goals.

But, who was my customer? The franchisee or the print job buyer?

I decided that the only answer to this question was to accept the franchisee as being my customer while never losing sight of who really is the backbone of my company – the consumer. My franchisee had to be trained to look after his own customers. The print consumer became our customer, not my customer. For this franchise to flourish, it was necessary that a win, win, win situation evolve for the customer, the franchisee and the franchisor.

Having made this conclusion, I realized I would be dividing my attention if I tried to run a printing business and provide support for my franchisees. I had to focus on one or the other. I chose to be a franchisor and, as it turned out, rightly so.

I recognized that the print buyer I was so keenly interested in would be best served if I could be The Best Darn Teacher and Consultant in the Franchise Business. I would give customers better service through highly skilled franchisees.

I had my goal, my vision and my will to make it happen.

## BUILDING A FOUNDATION

What Now? Where do I go from here?

First, let's assume that you have a printing business, know some special secrets or ways of doing things that make your job easier. Well it is time to get rid of the printing business to get on with your objective. You may have trouble leaving this lucrative source of funds for your new franchise direction, but it is absolutely essential that you relieve yourself of its day-to-day obligations. Why not hire a manager or for that matter, sell it to an employee as a franchise or a combination of both. You can retain controls of the initial showcase store as well as have an outlet to try new ideas, programs or equipment.

My suggestion, and I wish I had had the forethought initially, is that you set your sights twenty years down the road. Ask yourself, where do you want to be? How many stores? How profitable?

Take a look at the big picture. Allow yourself to dream. If you plan big, you will succeed big. It is that simple. Most people think small because they don't allow themselves to dream far enough into the future. Surely twenty years from now you can achieve your dream. As long as you have this dream, getting there should be very simple and methodical: one step at a time.

Now you can benchmark, or give yourself goals along the new voyage. For instance, in ten years where will you need to be in order to achieve or surpass your final twenty-year dream? Then cut this ten down to five – to two – to one – to half the year – to next month – next week. If you take this approach you will probably realize that your twenty-year dream is not so far fetched.

If you plan, it becomes easy to find your direction and not get off track.

## THE DREAM

In my business, we looked at the market potential throughout the world. Remember to start big. We recognized there was a universal need for printing. We decided every five hundred businesses would need a printing supplier who was close by and dedicated to service. We realized there was an established industry that would compete for our customers. However, we quickly grabbed a small percentage of their market. We also realized that customers would deal with us over any other source if we simply made it easier for them to do so.

We provided printing in less than one day, compared to the industry's norm of three weeks. This superior service attracted customers who were satisfied with good quality at reasonable prices.

We went to the post office twenty years ago and found that they broke down the postal codes into business or residential addresses. With this information we calculated that we had a potential market of 350 stores. We now have 83 centres or about 25% of our marketplace. Had we concentrated more on the dream or had the advice and support that is available today, perhaps we could have had 60%.

The truth of the matter is that we could have had 80% of the market niche, but we had set our sights too low in the 20-year plan and made a critical error by not revamping the 20-year plan at least every two years. We were not adjusting to our full potential of the dream.

People often talk about corporate culture. I believe it happens naturally in every good company. You can however, influence the speed at which it develops. Culture is the basis or philosophy of your business. It is the culmination of your mission statement.

Back to the dream. What do you want to be 20 years from now? In my case, it was being The Best Darn Teacher and Consultant in the Franchise Business. This became my mission statement and continues today in the company. In 1996, we were honoured by the Canadian Franchise Association with their "Award of Excellence." We were overwhelmed to be selected as the best franchise system in Canada. This honour really was a direct result of our simple mission statement. Our integrity, dedication, conviction, direction, methods and systems must always focus on our mission statement and all of these ingredients ultimately became the company's culture.

Our mission statement was always driven by providing customers with quality and service beyond their requirements. We focused on our mission, which meant developing standards by which we could teach and consult with our franchisees in a disciplined, constructive direction.

In addressing the profitability of a franchise business, we need to pay special attention to the sources of revenue available to franchisors. What are some of these sources of funds?

- A percentage royalty based on sales by a store.

- A fixed monthly levy charged each store.

- Profit on the sale of a store, or the franchise fee. (Initially Kwik Kopy Printing did not profit on the sale of a store. We relied strictly on royalty revenues for survival. Today through efficient purchasing, organization and market conditions, there is a marginal profitability in this area.)

- Supplier rebates based on volume purchases or commitments.

- A surcharge on supplies bought from head office by the franchisee.

- Charges for services provided (such as bookkeeping, advertising, accounting) or supplies (if sold to stores directly rather than through a vendor).

- Administration fee for handling the monthly premises rental or lease.

- Advertising fees (percentage of sales or fixed amount).

- Computer or networking fees.

- National account fee. This occurs when a franchisor negotiates a deal with a national account across the country involving each store's participation.

- Marketing fees. Sometimes a franchisor will do all of the sales functions and distribution functions from the head office.

- Training fees when franchisees or franchisees' staff needs upgrading.

- Seminar fees charged to attending franchisee.

- Conference registration fees.

- Leasehold improvement and signage fees.

Once the revenue stream or the source of your funds is established, you should decide what is a reasonable profit for the franchisor. Bearing in mind if the franchisee does not profit, you will not survive in the long run. In my opinion, a fair profit is typically the profit percentage equal to the profit achievable by a store. For instance, if a store's profit is realistically 25% of sales, then the franchisor profit should be 25% of the franchisees' revenue.

The balance left between the sales revenue and the projected profit is what you have available to spend to build your system. Initially these costs may be unbalanced. For example, you may need to advertise in the beginning in order to get your product known. This advertising amount will probably exceed your expected revenue for this item.

What is the vision for your stores? This is important because as you grow and change, you will expect the older franchisees to change with you as well. Therefore, it is beneficial if the leasehold images you adopted originally were good forever. However, this is also totally impractical. Give some thought to building an image that is basic and can be easily improved upon cosmetically when needed. A franchisee will not be overly excited about spending money on image changes every year.

Now banking becomes an important ingredient. You must have sufficient capital or collateral to support their involvement and be willing to gamble it against the borrowed funds. In the case of a Small Business Development Loan supported by the Government of Canada, this collateral requirement must be in place. An accountant or experienced franchise consultant can assist you in identifying these costs and help in the preparation of your business plan, both short and long term.

In my way of thinking, the growth of Kwik Kopy Printing would have been enormously quicker if there had been qualified experts available for consultation. Accountants and banks did not have an understanding or inclination as to how to deal with royalty revenues, which came to the franchisor without an invoice. It was a contractual sum and therefore, there was no receivable against which an amount could be anticipated or recognized. There were no acceptable receivables to record. Times have changed.

Lawyers treated franchising like a contract on an individual basis. There were no knowledgeable franchise legal advisors. Again, times have changed. Today there are valuable, experienced franchise consultants who can give you advice or direct you to the proper advisor.

In retrospect, I wish we had built a company from the "bottom up" rather than the "top down". The philosophy of "Total Quality Management" really works. About eight years ago we made changes in our company, which resulted in our becoming the first franchise company in the world to be ISO 9000 certified. This certification was not monetarily rewarding, but it allowed us to grow beyond our expectations. For instance, no one in our company has more contact with the franchisees than the telephone receptionist. Why not ask her opinion as to how the company should be run. It may sound silly, but it is the most rewarding and effective way of getting insight into your business. If I had known this management ideal was available in the 1970s, I would have implemented it immediately. My dreamtime would have been halved.

## ORGANIZATION

To be a good Teacher and Consultant, you need the following skills:

- Knowledge
- Understanding
- Experience
- Commitment
- Benchmarking

We had knowledge, however basic it was. The understanding of franchising would come as we grew. Experience was part of our success of getting to where we were at that point in time. The mission statement showed commitment.

However, the most important ingredient of all is people. It goes without saying you must surround yourself with people who accept and adapt everything they do within the company based on your mission statement and culture. If they don't fit, it is beneficial for both that you part company. You cannot afford not to.

The franchisee's experience and knowledge were also critical to our mission statement. We had to encourage their participation and involvement with our business direction. More on this later.

We decided that our business should be broken down into several areas: selling new stores - which later included reselling existing stores; supporting the new stores through training and existing stores through upgrading; and, finally, keeping track of all the business being done by the franchisees as well as our own affairs.

Today, our organizational chart is remarkably close to its initial concept.

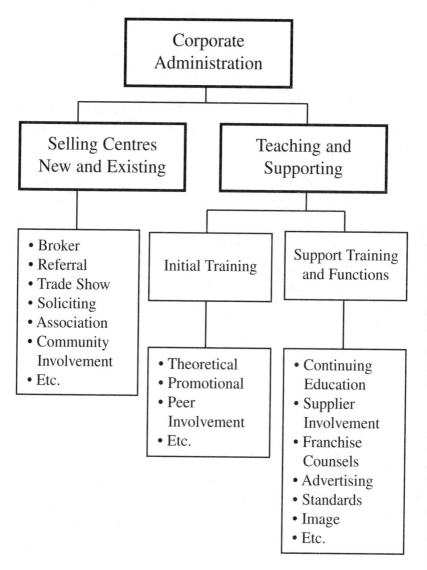

Initially we began with three people. I was in charge of the administrative side, which meant putting all the pieces in place. My partner was responsible for selling the stores, and we hired a secretary who gave us a professional image. Three people doing what is outlined in the bold borders. As the business grew, we acquired more employees who became experts in their respective fields and of course, clerical staff to keep things organized.

It became apparent that the corporate office staffing was directly proportionate to the number of centres we had. It amounted to one head office staff member for each five stores. This did not include the owners who helped us in some of the operations.

Today our head office organizational chart is very similar to the initial format. The philosophy we have always believed is – "A call from a new prospective franchisee is second to a call from an existing franchisee". We concentrated on support and growth of the existing owners. Thus, our support services grew in staff, but more importantly, in skilled personnel. We divided the major support disciplines needed by the franchisee into four areas:

- Sales – building of a customer base.

- Product – the production efficiencies required to be profitable.

- Network Technology – communication with head office and customers.

- Managing – controls required to run a good store (bookkeeping, benchmarking, etc.)

Our staff hired to concentrate in each discipline became experts very rapidly. More importantly, they began to recognize shortfalls in other disciplines and consequently, referred potential problems to the right advisors. Our response time to problems improved dramatically because we were identifying problems before they arose.

Another important philosophy that we implemented over ten years ago, which helped our business and influenced our organisation, was our commitment to communication. As we grew, we were confronted with problems, which directly related to communications. Fortunately we had a successful owner sell her business who we could contract to be our communicator. We now have three such consultants. The franchisees recognized that we listened to their concerns. . . .We began a program of contacting the franchisees monthly to find what they thought, felt and needed. Today, most of our successful programs originate with the franchisees, and are modified and developed by us. Our staff realizes that by nature the franchise business needs good communication above all else.

- What do they need to be more effective with the customer?
- What are the trends?
- What do the franchisees need?
- What is practical today?

To understand communication, we had to recognize that each franchisee was not a peg in a hole, but an individual. He needed tender loving care and to be reassured that we cared about his well-being. We accomplished this by having a weekly meeting where all the staff participated to clarify the lines of communications. The result was that everyone knew what was going on in the system. When anyone received a call from a franchisee, his needs were not lost between the cracks of our organization. This is a very important ingredient of being a good franchise.

# How do I Sell a Franchise?

As a starting point, consider that selling successfully relies mostly on your integrity. This one ingredient, in my opinion, will be the foundation of your system and success forever. The second you start misleading someone into buying a store, it is the beginning of the end of your business or more importantly, your dream.

Build integrity into everything you do. In the early going prospective franchisees asked many interesting questions, some that we had not even considered. We never let on that we knew everything, because we didn't. We listened to their questions and concerns, and answered them honestly. Often we simply said, "we don't know that answer, but what do you think?" This got the prospect involved with our program. They were appreciative of our honesty, sincerity and above all, integrity.

There are several alternatives open to you when you begin to promote the sale of your franchise. You can personally do the selling, hire an on-site sales person, or retain a broker. The Canadian Franchise Association has a list of franchise consultants for that purpose. However, choose your broker wisely. Remember what the broker says will reflect on your integrity.

In the Kwik Kopy Printing experience, we have used both methods (on-site sales representative and outside brokers) over the years. The brokerage method is less strenuous on your cash flow requirements because they are compensated once a sale is secured. A good broker however, will help you develop a proper sales and marketing plan and probably will want a modest retainer to cover minimal expenses. A good broker is worth their weight in gold providing they also are dedicated to integrity. Obviously the on-site sales person provides you with better controls, but is more costly initially. In my way of thinking, each alternative will probably cost you the same amount at the end of the day.

Selling a franchise is easy. Assessing and qualifying a prospective franchisee is difficult. In truth, during a sales presentation, you are really looking for more information about the prospect than he is about you.

- Do they fit your standards?
- Do they have ambition?
- Do they need support?
- Do they have the funding?
- Are they stable?

Furthermore, there are many reasons for a prospect to be seeking a franchise:

- To be their own boss.
- To control their own destiny.
- To build a base for their children.
- To secure their retirement.

Regardless of all these reasons, there is only one true motivational need – to make money.

You will constantly be asked, "How much money can I make?" The answer is you do not know. No one can answer that question with integrity. You can however, provide examples of what your present franchisees have achieved. It is very dangerous and unethical to embellish earnings. Avoid this situation. I have seen many franchises in trouble for not substantiating their forecasts.

At Kwik Kopy Printing, we begin our training process at the initial meeting. We consider it important that any businessperson fully understands the financial implications of the various aspects of his business. We basically begin that individual's business plan at the first meeting.

At this meeting we provide basic guidelines about the usual costs associated with running a store. The prospect is then encouraged to begin studying his own numbers to build a financial business plan. If the prospect will not produce an initial plan, we terminate further discussion. This may sound harsh, especially when we need new franchisees in the business, but experience tells us that a prospect must be interested in his own well being to be part of our system.

## REAL ESTATE

We consider real estate to be part of the sales and marketing department's responsibility. You want to establish what is needed for each prospect's store. Following is a list of items you may wish to consider:

- Territorial boundaries
- Exclusivity of territory
- Location - Downtown core area, suburban business park, retail environment, or Office tower
- Site search for space
- Visual impact of premises

- Leasehold improvements – responsibility of landlord, franchisee or franchisor?

- Lease held by whom? Franchisor or franchisee?

- Rent to be fixed or a percentage of sales volume?

- Signage requirements – product recognition

- Pedestrian traffic

- Motorized traffic

- Lease renewal policy

- Changing a location before end of lease

A very important decision must be made in the early stages of your business: how are you going to divide up the territories? Nationally? Provincial? By city, town or postal code, etc? This is a decision that will be difficult to rectify at a later stage. One lesson I learned was that although it is tempting to deviate, my growth should progress from local to regional to national. Otherwise, I could not effectively service my franchisees. I took the position that whatever support I provided locally must be available throughout the system, without any loss of quality.

We have had a real estate broker handle all of our site search programs since day one. He knows our needs and over the years, we have not had a poor location. As a precaution, our support team always has had final approval on every site.

## SUPPORT AND TRAINING

Training generally is an ongoing process requiring a structure to be followed throughout the term of the franchise. Initially, a franchisee must learn about your operational model.

Specific business training is probably most effective when done on a need to know basis. There is no need to confuse a new franchisee about a complicated product or device until he can effectively put this knowledge to use.

One problem with training is the retention of facts. A three-week training course requires deep concentration by the franchisee. Learning curves and retention are very different for each individual. We have found that being readily available to the franchisee after classroom training ends and hands on experience begins greatly assists the recall abilities and minimizes the learning period. Therefore, you must consider being closely involved with your franchisee immediately after training.

Each franchisee will need support in different areas. Some people need assistance training their employees. Others need accounting training. It might be counter productive training a franchisee with a background in accounting on accounting methods because he will feel that he should be concentrating on the areas where he really requires assistance. You should recognize the importance of involving the franchisee from the beginning in your training process and encourage his participation in building a better franchise.

Manuals are an important part of your system. Your franchisees will refer to them constantly. After the initial training, changes will inevitably occur and it is important to advise your existing franchisee of these changes. Therefore, continuous upgrading must be provided to ensure your entire franchisee network is working together. Initially you can advise of change by replacing manuals or through a newsletter.

This brings us to communication, which is among the most critical areas of support franchisees require. Initially a franchisee will need help getting started. But as time passes and confidence builds, the franchisee will have his own ideas to contribute. One saying, which I believe is imperative to your system, is: "We have two ears and one mouth – use them proportionately." Communication is more listening than telling. Your franchisee will assist you if you will listen. Sometimes their advice is self-centred, but peer involvement with other franchisees will likely dampen this inclination.

The main value of communication to a seasoned franchisee is involvement in the system as a peer. The best forum for this participation is through advisory committees. In Kwik Kopy Printing we have committees for advertising, supplier negotiation, etc. However, more importantly, we have a franchisee association, which meets on a regular basis and advises the head office of their needs, wishes and makes suggestions on improving the system. Everyone realizes that the stronger the system, the more advantageous it is to be a member.

One thing I learned through experience is that your support team must be involved in the selection process of a franchisee at an early stage. If they do not accept the franchisee, it will be difficult to be committed to the success of that individual. Likewise, allow their input into site and location decisions and supplier choices. Dedication by your staff is directly related to their acceptance of principles within your system.

## SALES SUPPORT

While reading this section, please remember that you must build a program to attract customers to your franchisee's business. Basically you have two areas of concentration in building sales.

- How to get new customers?
- How to keep existing customers?

Some say it is ten times easier to keep an old customer than to get a new one. Perhaps this is so. I do know however that giving a customer more than he expects will get him back. It is not hard to keep a customer if you determine what it is that makes him happy. We have used many approaches in Kwik Kopy Printing. One such program was called "You're worth a mint to us". We simply put a Kwik Kopy mint candy in with every invoice. The customer loved it and it brought them back again and again. That little bit extra did not cost very much, yet was "worth a mint". You must address a solution for your franchisees to adopt which will keep them coming back.

There are many reasons for a customer coming to you in the first place. He may be attracted to your advertising or he may have received a referral. Your location might be convenient, or your signage may have caught his attention. The important thing to remember is that no one method works for everyone. You must use a wide scope of recruiting methods to be successful.

Media advertising is obviously a very good way of reaching many people. Because of their large market, they are very expensive and you may not be able to afford them in your early stages of growth. The best approach is to identify the customer. Who he or she is, what age group, where are they, what income bracket? Once your customer boundaries are identified, then a very sophisticated mailing list can be rented for direct mail promotion. An advertising agency, direct mail house, or even your local printer can help you build such a program. The benefit is that it can be repeated in territories around the country, but also added to when improvements are identified. Advertising does not have to be expensive to be effective.

As your franchisee numbers grow, you should encourage the group to be part of a committee that will offer advice for your advertising program. Bear in mind that everyone considers himself to be an expert when it comes to advertising. The truth of that matter is that when it comes to advertising meetings, the franchisees will realize everyone has a different opinion and no time. They will then accept a professional, knowledgeable representative in advertising who can build a program based on input from the group. In this way, you are involving the franchisee in your system. Ultimately the advertising fund will be able to support a full time employee.

The advertising fund should be based on the number of franchisees as well as in relation to sales revenues. At Kwik Kopy Printing we use 3% of sales and we have found this to be realistic in our business.

Another tool to build sales is to provide incentive programs to your franchisees. Remember, each franchisee is different and driven by different motivators. Some will want money as the reward, others will want recognition, and others will want to provide their staff with a memorable reward for achievement. You must provide an incentive program that meets these criteria. It is difficult to combine into one program, so why not have three or four different programs?

Another way to attract customers is for the franchisees to become involved in community services. This can be considered as public relations under the advertising umbrella. Be specific as to what qualifies as PR. For that matter, be very specific as to what qualifies as advertising. For instance, does packaging count as promotion?

In our business, we encourage new franchisees to build a customer base of small business users. We then have programs of additional training in customer support, which result in certification levels as they progress. In this way, they are equipped to handle a sophisticated customer at the proper time of their growth. We had a franchisee committee build and contribute to their program. It would not have been effective if we had tried to develop it at head office. Use your franchisees' abilities to strengthen your system.

## PRODUCTION AND SUPPLY SUPPORT

This is where the technical side of the business rests. There can be no rest in this area. Things constantly change and you must be on top of it.

Suppliers are an important part of any business. When you are beginning, you will need someone who is able to respond quickly to your needs because you cannot afford to store, warehouse or carry a large inventory. Suppliers are an integral part of your business. Consequently, we choose people in the close vicinity to our office. But what about the stores? Are you going to distribute from head office or will the franchisee deal directly with the vendor? When you move into a regional market, away from the local area, will the supplier be able to service your requirements? How about nationally?

The supply area is another excellent opportunity for the franchisee to be involved with the franchise system. They know their needs and the suppliers will encourage their input. We have a "National Negotiating Committee" made up of owners who meet under our supervision semi-annually, to discuss their needs with vendors. Most times these needs do not concentrate on price, but service and quality are the key issues. One important area to cover in any negotiation with suppliers is what happens when a franchisee leaves the system? Be sure that this never happens, but if it should, be sure the franchisee is not able to benefit from your supply arrangements outside of the system.

Your operational staff is responsible for policing and monitoring the system. They will generally organize any field visits. We have a silent shopper program, which tests each centre's ability to cater to the customer. They monitor the image and quality of product. Generally, focus groups - meetings to find what truly is happening at the customer level - are carried out semi-annually. This department handles customer and franchisee grievances, operating shortfalls and creates solutions to concerns. They communicate directly with the other departments to maintain, correct and improve the system.

## BUSINESS MANAGEMENT SUPPORT

These are the resources required by every business to monitor results, identify trends, handle personnel and generate profits. Your franchisees will probably lack these specific skills but they can be acquired. It is your job to build this aptitude.

You probably will want every franchisee to use the same systems in order that everyone is aware of what is being addressed. This is also critical when owners are together (at conferences/seminars, etc.) to provide common ground for discussion. If everyone is on the same system, benchmarking can be extremely meaningful. Bookkeeping, accounting, networking with head office, between franchises and even with the customer should all be done through a common software network. Reporting is easier and timely.

*It is critical that revenue and expense from the sale of new franchises be separated from revenue and expense of ongoing operations.*

Franchisors must perform all of the monitoring of the financial matters pertaining to the franchise network. They monitor sales locally, regionally and nationally on a basis of dollar amount, product mix, profit margin and sales to staff ratios. After a period of time, you will see training direction, sales consultation, etc. You will become sophisticated as to how to build areas of high profitability for your franchisees.

The main importance of financial reporting is to understand where the revenue is coming from and on what function expenses are being spent. There are two main sources of profit: new franchisees and the royalty. Unless recorded and reported separately, the franchisor may be misled into thinking more profit is being generated than really is. This is particularly true in a period of ongoing high new franchise sales.

A good financial statement is based on a simple chart of account that separates sources of revenue and cost of revenue, and departmentalises expenses into major functions within the organization. Financial statements should be kept simple and concise in order that all management is able to review and understand the results. It is important that reports include at least six months and year-to-date statements, rather than the conventional monthly and year-to-date format. Trend analysis is more significant than a point-in-time view in franchising.

Profit on sales of new franchises should not be recorded in the income statement until such time as the sale and costs (including start-up expenses) are complete. Record deposits, revenue and all expenses in separate balance sheet accounts for each new franchise. This will allow you to determine profit on new centres by geographic area or type of sale.

A by-product of the invoicing system should allow the reporting of centre sales by category. This is important not only to franchise operations, but also to determine what is happening in the market place so that you are better able to budget future royalty revenue.

As a franchisor, it is important to understand that your profits are totally dependent on the performance of the franchisees. You are not "master of your own destiny" other than through the efforts of the operations and marketing departments, and only then to the extent that the franchisee is willing to follow instructions.

It is critical that revenue and expense from the sale of new franchises be separated from revenue and expense of ongoing operations. Otherwise you may get a false sense of long-term security when looking at your overall performance during the growth periods of selling new franchises.

The factors that will affect your profit are:

- Financial Health of franchisee
- Franchisee's Sales
- Economic Conditions
- Technological Changes
- Sales Mix of Franchises
- Collection of Fees
- Monitoring Overhead in Relation to Expected Royalty
- Seasonality of the Industry

The main purpose for franchise monitoring is to ensure reporting and payment of royalties and advertising fees. Franchise monitoring within the context of the franchisor's administration function is geared to the franchisor's profit rather than the franchisee.

## CONCLUSION

Does this seem monumental to you – not at all? If you begin with "the Dream," everything falls into place as you proceed along your game plan. I believe if you involve your owners and staff and make it easy for them to be successful, you cannot miss.

Franchising is a great industry because it provides the "win, win, win" results. It is exciting, vibrant and rewarding to all involved. Don't be overly concerned with the challenges of reaching your dream. Challenges and obstacles are part of the voyage. You step over them one at a time on your quest to making your dream a reality.

In conclusion, if I had to do it over again I would have built a support system for the following areas right from the start:

### A. *Long Term*

- Define the end result of the dream
- Develop a mission statement
- Create an environment which always has a franchisee dependency curve
- Build a long term organizational chart
- Build a total quality management system

## B. *Short Term*

- Constantly build and refine a business plan to achieve the dream.

- Encourage franchisee involvement from day one

- Join and be involved in community and industry associations

- Emphasize franchise support to franchisees

- Recruit franchisees who want to exit the business within ten years in order that the business can continue to grow after that term

- Provide full integrity to franchisees, staff and vendors

- Establish consultant connections

- Budget business plan for strong, initial recruiting

- Review territory expansion locally, regionally and nationally

- Build a site selection process

- Develop good initial marketing program to build customers

- Develop ways of keeping old customers

- Build advertising and promotion plan

- Create an award incentive program to encourage, involve and reward franchisees

- Provide franchisees with good and meaningful training both initially and as they grow and progress

- Teach and insist on quality of product

- Teach and insist on good accounting practices

- Build a strong review system to assist franchisee growth

- Monitor and take action on infractions in the system image and delinquent payment to you

- Protect and feed your corporate culture

# ABOUT THE AUTHORS

 ## ROBERT (BOB) BOUGIE

Bob Bougie is a Partner with Deloitte & Touche LLP and a Senior Vice President of Deloitte & Touche Inc.

As a senior practitioner in the firm's Financial Advisory Services practice and retail industry sector leader for the Greater Toronto Area, Bob has been involved in numerous retail and franchise related assignments. Prior to joining Deloitte & Touche, Bob acted as CFO to one of Canada's largest retail chains.

Bob holds a BPE from McMaster University, a BCom from the University of Windsor, a C.A. designation, a Trustee in Bankruptcy license and is a Chartered Insolvency & Restructuring Professional and a Certified Fraud Examiner.

## KENT HARDING

Kent Harding is the Chairman and Founding CEO of Kwik Kopy Printing Canada Corporation, which entered the Canadian market in 1979, where it presently has in excess of 80 outlets serving Canadian businesses.

In addition, Kent is the Chairman of Kwik Kopy International Ltd., which is the international development arm of Kwik Kopy Printing, responsible for extension of the services of Kwik Kopy Printing around the world. Kent travels extensively throughout the world, meeting with License Holders to discuss successful approaches to common challenges.

Having in excess of 1000 centres in twenty-one countries, Kwik Kopy Printing is the international leader in its industry.

Kent was born and raised in Toronto, Canada. His then, 65 year old grandfather, Harold, began in the printing business at the beginning of the depression. Rough times followed, but determination prevailed and the business grew into Canada's largest display manufacturing company. Kent remains on the board of this Corporation, but presently dedicates his attention to the pursuit of the Kwik Kopy Printing Franchise System.

Kent was educated in Canada, graduating from Ryerson College in Business Administration. He is married with two children, who also follow the Harding tradition and are very involved in the family business.

Kent enjoys skiing, golf, cycling and painting.

# RAJIV MATHUR

Rajiv Mathur is a Partner with Deloitte & Touche LLP and heads the Franchise Services group in Canada.

As a Partner in the firm's Assurance and Advisory practice, Rajiv has been involved in providing a variety of professional services to franchising, retail, and consumer product manufacturing and distribution client.

Rajiv is a member of the CFA's communication committee. He has been a speaker on several occasions at the Canadian Franchise Associations Annual conventions. Mr. Mathur has published articles on a number of franchising topics.

Rajiv holds an MBA from Queens University and a CA from Ontario.

## G. LEE MUIRHEAD

G. Lee Muirhead was called to the Ontario Bar in 1985. She is a partner in the Business Law Department of Osler, Hoskin & Harcourt LLP where she has practised since 1986.. Her practice focuses on franchising, licensing, intellectual property, distribution, marketing, and trade practice law, including trade secrets, consumer protection, advertising, and packaging and labelling. She has written articles and presented papers on franchising, trade-mark, copyright and advertising matters including for the Canadian Bar Association of Ontario, Insight, the Canadian Franchise Association, the American Bar Association Forum on Franchising, the International Trade-mark Association, Infonex, Canadian Corporate Counsel, Franchise Law Journal and Franchise Voice. She is a member of the Canadian Bar Association, the American Bar Association, the Canadian Franchise Association and the International Franchise Association.

## MAC VOISIN

Mac Voisin was born and raised in the Kitchener-Waterloo area. He graduated from the University of Waterloo as a mechanical engineer in 1973. He couldn't find employment, so chose instead to sell real estate until 1976. At that time, he and his brother Greg set up a construction company to build houses.

Then in June 1980, Mac and his then brother-in-law Mark Nowak (hence M&M) became frustrated with the lack of quality, convenient food products being offered in the marketplace, so they set up their first M&M Meat Shop in Kitchener in October 1980. Mark left the company in 1985 to return to his law practice. Today, there are 329 stores across Canada.

M&M Meat Shops has received the highest awards in the food and franchise industries, including their most recent in December as a winner of Canada's 50 Best Managed Companies 2001 (sponsored by Andersen, CIBC, National Post and Queen's School of Business). M&M raises millions of dollars each year for various charities across Canada, and the Crohn's & Colitis Foundation of Canada is their corporate charity of record.

## LARRY WEINBERG

Mr. Weinberg is a partner at the Toronto law firm of Cassels Brock & Blackwell LLP where he practices in the area of franchising and intellectual property law, with specific experience in all forms of franchising, licensing, information technology, trademarks, and the distribution of goods and services. He has been a speaker at, and organiser of, various legal and business related conferences on licensing, distribution and franchising, and a speaker on small business and franchising, on radio and television. He is an active member of the American Bar Association's Forum on Franchising, the International Bar Association's Committee X (Franchising), and the Canadian Franchise Association. Both he and Cassels Brock & Blackwell LLP are listed in the Lexpert™ legal directory as among the leaders in Canada in franchise law. In 1999 the CFA bestowed upon him its "Special Recognition Award" given "in recognition of outstanding support and contribution to the Canadian Franchise Association and the franchising community".

## John Woodburn

John is the President and founder of C.J. Woodburn & Associates - a franchise consulting firm. He has been involved in the franchise industry since 1975. During this time he has served as:

- President and C.O.O. of a start-up franchise system.
- Owner and operator of a master franchise system.
- Vice-President and Director of Franchising for franchise systems.

During the past ten years, his company has specialized in helping new and established franchisors market their systems and expand regionally, nationally and internationally. This has involved work throughout North America, plus special assignments in Europe and as far away as Saudi Arabia.

# WHO WE ARE

## THE CFA REPRESENTS FRANCHISE EXCELLENCE

---

### Canadian Franchise Association's Mission Statement
*"To promote and exemplify franchise excellence through
a national association of businesses united by a
common interest in ethical franchising."*

---

The Canadian Franchise Association is a national trade association of franchisors including Canada's leading franchise systems, all committed to achieving excellence in franchising. Our membership represents a diverse cross-section of franchisors in Canada, ranging from very large established systems to smaller regional concepts.

*But Not Everyone Qualifies for Membership*

The CFA restricts membership to only those franchisors who commit to adhering to its Code of Ethics and mandatory disclosure requirements. Prospective members are carefully screened to be certain they meet the high franchising standards maintained by our membership.

*Members fall into three categories:*

Regular Members:
Companies that have been in the business of franchising for two years or longer in Canada.

Associate Members: Companies that have been franchising for less than two years in Canada.

Franchise Support
Service Members:
Companies that provide products and services to the franchising sector such as law firms, banks, designers, marketing firms, etc.

Our members proudly display the CFA logo as a signal to customers and prospective franchisees that they strive to achieve excellence in franchising. "Each of our members has their own reasons for belonging to the CFA - but overwhelmingly they agree that they are better franchisors as a result of their experience in the organization."

## 30 Years of Franchise Excellence

The Canadian Franchise Association was founded in 1967 by a small group of franchisors who saw the need for a national organization committed to the growth, enhancement and development of ethical franchising throughout Canada.

## Advocacy

The CFA is the voice of franchising in Canada and has been very successful in establishing fruitful relationships with all levels of government to ensure the development of "industry-made" solutions.

"The CFA receives thousands of calls from potential franchisees wanting to know whether or not their prospective franchisor is a member of the CFA and what membership means."

## Education

Franchising is not the kind of business you can learn "on the job". The CFA delivers a variety of seminars and networking events nationaly throughout the year providing practical insights into almost every aspect of franchising. These programs provide an opportunity for the sharing of problems and solutions with colleagues in the franchise industry.

## Information

CFA members receive The Franchise Voice, the Association's newsletter, featuring articles about issues important to Canadian franchisors, updates on legal and business issues, success stories and member profiles.

## Franchise Canada

The Canadian Franchise Association is the proud publisher of Franchise Canada Magazine, a bi-monthly periodical, and Franchise Canada Directory, the official directory of the CFA. Both publications offer first-rate articles on franchise trends and industry leaders, invaluable advice for franchise investors, insider business columns by the CFA's industry experts, plus much more. Check your local newsstand for the latest issue of Canada's best franchise industry publications or order direct from the CFA.

## The Franchise Show

The Franchise Show is Canada's largest franchisor-only show produced by the CFA. This show offers individuals interested in purchasing a franchise the opportunity to attend free seminars, browse through our exhibitor's booths and talk to the experts one-on-one about one of Canada's fastest growing business sectors.

**To learn more about the Canadian Franchise Association and the Canadian Franchise Industry, contact:**

**Telephone: (905) 625-2896 • Toll-free: (800) 665-4232
Website: www.cfa.ca**

# GLOSSARY OF TERMS

## Business Format Franchising

A form of franchising where the franchisor provides the specific method or system for running the franchised business based on prescribed operation practices, with continuing control by the franchisor over the uniformity and quality of the operations

## Copyright

The ownership of rights over any manuals, written materials or other published materials within your system

## Corporate Locations

Franchisor owned locations

## Entrepreneur

A person who undertakes an enterprise or business, with the chance of profit or loss

## Franchise

The right to use the trade-marks, know-how and business systems of the franchisor, and to promote and market products and/or services using such, trademarks, know – how and systems.

## Franchisee

The company or person who contracts with the franchisor for the right to operate the franchise in return for a payment of an initial fee and/or an ongoing royalty

## Franchising

A way of doing business in which the franchisor gives the franchisee the right to offer, sell or distribute goods or services identified by the franchisor's trade- mark

### Franchisor

The company or individual that owns or controls the trade-marks and the franchise system and grants the right to operate the franchise using the trademarks, know – how and business systems of the franchisor

### Initial or Up-Front Fee

A one-time fee paid by the franchisee to the franchisor in payment for the right to operate a franchised business (also known as a franchise fee or license fee)

### Multiple Franchising

A form of business format franchising, which covers more than one unit including:

**Area/ Multiple Unit Franchisee** - A franchisor licenses a franchisee to operate more than one outlet within a defined area based on a development schedule

**Master or Sub-Franchising** - A three-tiered structure in which a franchisor gives a franchisee the right to grant unit franchisees to sub-franchisees within a defined area

### Royalty or Service Fee

An ongoing fee paid by the franchisee to the franchisor usually calculated as a percentage of sales

### Renewal Fee

A fee paid by the franchisee at the end of a term of the franchise agreement for renewing the franchise agreement

### Trade-Mark

A name, symbol or other device identifying a product or services of the franchisor which distinguishes them from similar products and services supplied by third parties